Also Available from Bloomsbury:

Forensic Linguistics: Second Edition
John Olsson

Where Words Come From
Fred Sedgwick

Language: The Big Picture
Peter Sharpe

Understanding Language: Second Edition
Elizabeth Grace Winkler

Language and The Law
Sanford Schane

The 'Language Instinct' Debate
Geoffrey Sampson

The Grammar Detective
Gillian Hanson

The Language of The Third Reich
Victor Klemperer

WORDCRIME

SOLVING CRIME THROUGH FORENSIC LINGUISTICS

John Olsson

Bloomsbury Academic
An imprint of Bloomsbury Publishing Plc

B L O O M S B U R Y

LONDON · OXFORD · NEW YORK · NEW DELHI · SYDNEY

Bloomsbury Academic
An imprint of Bloomsbury Publishing Plc

50 Bedford Square
London
WC1B 3DP
UK

1385 Broadway
New York
NY 10018
USA

www.bloomsbury.com

BLOOMSBURY and the Diana logo are trademarks of Bloomsbury Publishing Plc

First published in 2009 by the Continuum International Publishing Group Ltd
This paperback edition published 2012
Reprinted by Bloomsbury Academic 2013, 2014, 2015, 2017 (twice)

British Library Cataloguing-in-Publication Data
A catalogue record for this book is available from the British Library.

ISBN: PB: 978-1-4411-9352-0
        ePDF: 978-0-8264-3443-2
        ePub: 978-1-4725-3880-2

Library of Congress Cataloging-in-Publication Data
A catalog record for this book is available from the Library of Congress.

Typeset by Newgen Imaging Systems Pvt Ltd, Chennai, India
Printed and bound in Great Britain

CONTENTS

INTRODUCTION

What is forensic linguistics? If you have gotten this far, it is a question that you may have some answers to already. On the other hand, forensic linguistics might be a subject that you have heard nothing on, but want to know more about.

My name is John Olsson, and for the past 15 years I have been (and still am) the world's only full-time forensic linguist. This book concerns my work, and is designed in part to illustrate how forensic linguistics can help solve crime. Before I move onto this though, I would like to go over some background information. Let me detail in brief how the science of forensic linguistics came into being.

In 1968 a Swedish linguist working at the University of London heard about a case which had occurred a number of years previously. It concerned the murder of several women and a baby at an infamous London address, 10 Rillington Place, Kensington. Rillington Place became so notorious that the authorities were eventually forced to change its name to Ruston Close at the request of the people who lived there. However, the bad associations remained and eventually the local council demolished the entire street and a new development of houses was constructed there in the 1970s.

The ground-floor tenant of 10 Rillington Place was one John Christie, a quiet perhaps even shy man, apparently contentedly married. Above him lived Timothy Evans and his wife Beryl and their baby daughter. Evans disappeared from Rillington Place in 1949 and questions began to be asked about the whereabouts of his wife and baby. In November of that year, Evans handed himself into police in South Wales where he had been living with his uncle at Merthyr Tydfil. Forensic linguistics comes into the story at this point because Evans was supposed to have given several statements to the police confessing to the crime. Evans was found guilty partly on the basis of the statements and partly on the basis of evidence given by John Christie. Evans was hanged in 1950. Later Christie's wife disappeared and neighbours began asking questions about his odd behaviour. After Christie moved out another tenant occupied his flat and, while attempting to put up a shelf made a gruesome discovery: a partly clothed woman's body. When police arrived at the house they found evidence of several other murders. Christie was eventually tracked down, charged, found guilty and later hanged. Not long before he died he confessed to the murder of Evans' wife and 'probably' of their baby. Despite urgent requests to investigate these claims before Christie's execution date the Home Secretary refused to halt the hanging and Christie was put to death in July 1953. The crimes he had confessed to for which Evans had been hanged continued to be attributed to Evans for over a decade until journalist Ludovic Kennedy became interested in the case in the 1960s and the statements also drew the attention of a Swedish professor working at the University of London. Jan Svartvik examined the statements and concluded that they contained not one but several styles of language, most of which were written in what is known as 'policeman's register'. Svartvik's analysis and the unwavering campaign by Kennedy caused the Home Secretary to reverse the conviction and Evans was posthumously pardoned. This was probably the first murder appeal in the world in which linguistics played a prominent part. Because Svartvik used the term 'forensic linguistics' in his report on the statements he is credited with being the 'father' of the discipline.

In the 1990s the case of Derek Bentley drew the attention of linguists at Birmingham University where I was doing postgraduate research in linguistics. Several anomalies appeared in the statement Bentley is supposed to have dictated to police officers after the shooting of Police Constable Sidney Miles at a burglary in South London by Bentley's co-burglar, Chris Craig. A number of other previously accepted confessions now fell under suspicion and one after another several convictions were quashed, largely on the basis of evidence provided by ESDA trace, an electrostatic procedure which has certain elements in common with photocopying and reveals indentations from other sheets if several sheets were placed on top of each other in the course of writing.

In 1994 I founded the Forensic Linguistics Institute in the United Kingdom which has since become one of the leading linguistics laboratories in the world. Along with my colleagues I examine texts of all types for authorship, authenticity, interpretation of meaning, disputed language and other forensic processes. An early case involved the analysis of an alleged terrorist's statement to police at Paddington Green Police Station in the mid-1980s. Since that time I have handled nearly 300 forensic linguistics investigations. These have ranged from examining the language of suicide letters for genuineness, assessing threat in extortion demands, evaluating police interview tapes for alleged oppressive interviewing (a rare occurrence these days), and the authorship identification of many hundreds of letters, emails and mobile phone texts in a range of inquiries from murder to extortion to witness intimidation, sexual assault and internet child pornography. I get commissioned by police forces, solicitors, international companies and organizations, and even private clients who have received hate mail from someone who might live just down the road or even next door.

In an early case I was asked by the president of a dog club in the midwest of the United States to see whether a spate of hate mail letters the club had received came from one of their own members. The most likely author turned out to be an elderly mild-mannered lady who had devotedly carried out the club's administrative affairs for many years, but who had been disappointed by the failure of one of her pets to win a prize at the club's annual dog show. It may come as something of a surprise, but hate mail also occurs within families: in one case a disgruntled woman had become infuriated at the success of her younger brother in his hotel business and wrote a spate of poison letters to the local chamber of commerce not only denigrating his efforts but insulting his wife, accusing him of nazism and claiming that the hotel often hosted white supremacist weekends. In another case a teenage girl grew jealous of her sister's impending marriage and tried to poison her against the bridegroom. On the other hand, not all hate mail is from family members: I recently had to attempt an identification in which a middle-aged male, having been sexually rebuffed by a teenage boy, then wrote to the boy's parents accusing their son of being a child molester. The boy's father – perhaps as a result of this accusation against what he perceived to be his family's honour – then committed suicide.

However, there is something you the reader should know, in case you are ever the victim of hate mail, or in case you receive hate mail which denigrates a friend, relative or colleague: in every hate mail case I have dealt with the accusation has turned out to be pure malice – a complete invention. Yet these inventions are capable of wrecking lives, as I have seen all too often. A businessman of my acquaintance received several such letters and it nearly destroyed him, even though he – and everyone around him – knew that the accusations contained in those letters were completely false. It was only through strong family support that he was eventually able to recover. The perpetrator of this terrible crime – and you only have to see the effect on people's lives to realize how serious a crime it is – has never been found.

Nor should anyone imagine, as per those dark 1940s and 1950s films, that all hate mail writers are women. Far from it: rancour and spite know no gender boundaries, no age limits and no social divisions. I have seen hate mail from young teenagers, old aristocrats and middle-aged artisans, from highly successful executives, doctors, and respectable grandparents. The internet has enabled the genre to flourish: anybody can access a free email address under a pseudonym and post the vilest slander about another person on public forums or communicate it privately in emails. However, despite the advent of technology, the Royal Mail and other postal services around the world still deliver thousands of traditionally written paper missives every day, each designed to destroy a happy life, wreck a worthy reputation or sow the seeds of hatred between formerly devoted couples or other family members. The motive is not always hatred either: it is often a combination of boredom and a failure to foresee the inevitable devastation which can occur.

Fortunately, forensic linguistics is not all hate mail cases. Every day brings a unique inquiry: the father who wants to know if the letter he has received from his daughter is really in her style, the mother who is concerned her teenager's writing is becoming influenced by 'gang speak', the insurance company trying to identify a fraudster's voice from among several possible clients, the police detective trying to interpret a coded letter from a prisoner to an accomplice, the prisoner who claims innocence, the solicitor working on an appeal for her client, the employee who feels his bosses are trying to frame him by saying he wrote an anonymous email – the list is seemingly endless.

In the 15 years I have been doing this work I have analysed literally thousands of texts by hundreds of different writers implicated in scores of types of crime. In that time forensic linguistics has grown from being a marginal discipline which only a few people were passionate about to an internationally recognized practice which can be of real service to law enforcement and the legal profession.

In this book I will show you the details of some of the many cases I have been privileged to work on. Wherever possible I have avoided identifying victims, where they live or what their occupations are or were. This has sometimes also meant that I could not identify the perpetrators of some of these crimes either. Unfortunately, some cases are well-known to the public and could not be anonymized, and the reader who follows the daily news will recognize these cases quite easily. Some cases are too recent to write about, but I hope to be able to do so in years to come when memories of certain crimes and events are no longer fresh in the public memory.

I hope that this book, which tells the stories of many lives, mostly of ordinary people often faced with extraordinary circumstances through no choice of their own, will show you the power of language analysis in the solving of crime. In telling you about these lives in a simple narrative format I have tried to do so in a straightforward, down-to-earth way. My aim is not primarily to tell a 'good story', but to illustrate how interesting and complex language is, and how powerful a resource it can be when it enters the arena of the law. If the stories are worth reading I hope this will not be seen as in any way lessening the importance or the tragedy of the events they seek to describe. I am always conscious of the fact that the work is about people above all, and not just language, and I have found this to be both a privilege and a responsibility over the years.

Forensic linguistics began life as an instrument to correct miscarriages of justice. It now plays an active day-to-day role in our courts. The common law system which has evolved in England, Wales, Scotland and Ireland in the last millennium should be treasured by all who live in these islands, despite its undoubted errors over the years. This is why forensic science is so important. In an age when the erosion of civil rights and liberties has once again become a topic to rouse the passions, and rightly so, forensic science stands as one of the guardians of justice and liberty. From small beginnings just 40 years ago, forensic linguistics is now an important, and I believe, permanent component in this process.

Part 1

1

THE BARREL KILLER

Julie Turner was just 40 years old when she went missing in Yorkshire one summer evening in 2005. She was known as an attractive mother of two, and lived in Sheffield. On Tuesday, 7th June at about 6 p.m. she left her home to go shopping with Howard Simmerson, a man she had been having an affair with for 4 years. When she left home her partner Darren knew that she would be with Simmerson. Julie was not discreet about her relationship, and neighbours often saw his Mercedes in the vicinity as he picked her up or dropped her off. The couple even used to collect her children from school together.

Simmerson lived in Creswell, Derbyshire, which is about 20 miles south of Sheffield. By 11 p.m. that evening Julie still had not returned and Darren was getting increasingly worried. He decided to drive down to Simmerson's house. The Mercedes was parked outside, but the house was in darkness and there was no sign of Simmerson. In frustration Darren drove back home. Four hours later, at 3.22 a.m. on Wednesday morning, he finally reported Julie as missing. Inquiries were made at local hospitals, and family members were contacted, but there was still no trace of Julie.

The following afternoon Darren received a mobile phone text, as follows:

Stopping at jills, back later need to sort my head out

Darren could not understand this text as he was not aware of anyone called Jill, Julie never texted on her phone, and he did not know the mobile number from which the text was sent. Moreover, he knew that Julie was always concerned about her children, and would never go anywhere without telling them where she would be.

Later that evening he and several members of his family went to Creswell again. A fire was burning in the grounds of Simmerson's home and the two men spoke. Simmerson was somewhat dismissive and Darren left Creswell no wiser as to Julie's whereabouts. The following day Darren received another message on his mobile phone:

Tell kids not to worry. sorting my life out. be in touch to get some things

The next day at about 2 p.m., police officers visited Simmerson at his business premises in Chesterfield. He was not in the office and a member of staff contacted him on his mobile telephone. One of the officers spoke to Simmerson who stated that he could be back in the office in half an hour or so.

After some considerable delay, a further call was made to him asking how much longer he would be and he explained that he had been held up by roadworks. He arrived at about 3.30 p.m. in a Ford Ranger vehicle.

The officers found him helpful. He was quite open about his desire that Julie should leave Darren and live with him. The officers requested that he hand over his mobile phone. He actually had two – one exclusively for his contact with Julie, and the other for his business.

On one of the phones there was a message, apparently from Julie, received the previous evening:

Sucker.im stopping at my friends.guess who. why do you think i wanted to rush back. dont bother looking for me.

Looking at these phone texts there is not much to go on. In cases involving written or word-processed texts – instead of mobile phone texts – you usually have anything up to a dozen letters, each several hundred words long. Even samples of that size are not always easy to work with, and you will often hear linguists complaining of 'sample size' as being a factor in preventing identification. However, by comparison with the present case, a sample of that size seemed luxurious.

Nevertheless, there are several points of possible similarity. One interesting feature of the mobile phone texts is the use of a full stop instead of a comma: 'Sucker.im stopping at my friends.' In this situation we would expect a comma rather than a full stop after the word 'sucker'.

In the meantime, police had found a five-page letter from Simmerson at his home. They seized the letter. It did not appear to be addressed to anyone. In it there was mention of a gun he wanted to buy from someone called 'Mike'. From the letter it appeared that Simmerson intended to kill himself and Julie.

There were several examples in the letter of a full stop being used as a comma, just as in the text example above:

Well. a week on Since my first letter of disaster

Oh god what a tangle. but she is not getting away with my life

On its own, however, this feature offered little help: this is because there is no way of estimating the frequency with which people would use a full stop instead of a comma. All I could say was that it *seemed* rare. I didn't know *how* rare.

There was little else in the phone texts. However, I was interested in the word 'sort', as seen in the two phone texts above:

Stopping at jills, back later need to <u>sort</u> my head out

Tell kids not to worry. <u>sorting</u> my life out. be in touch to get some things

I asked officers for a copy of the interview tapes, and listened to them carefully for several hours. There was very little. Then, just when I was about to turn the tape off for the day, I heard one of the officers ask a question about the relationship between Simmerson and Julie, and why the couple were not living together since it seemed to be something they both wanted. Simmerson replied:

She was on heavy medication and she said when she'd got her head <u>sorted</u> out and <u>sorted</u> her life out then it would happen.

This stunned me and I had to play the section several times to make sure I had really heard what I thought I had heard: 'head sorted out . . . sorted her life out'. The two phrases 'sorting one's head out' and 'sorting one's life out' are actually quite unusual: one reason for this perhaps is that not many people would actually admit to their life being so bad or difficult that they would have to 'sort' it out. Certainly, 'sorting things out' or 'sorting everything out' are not uncommon, but 'sorting' one's *life* out and 'sorting' one's *head* out are much rarer. At the time I found only one instance of 'sort my life out' in a 100 million word corpus (a collection of language). There was also one instance of 'sorted his life out', and no instances of 'sorted my life out' or 'sort his/her life out'. There were no instances of 'sort ~ head out'. Google gave 23,000 instances of 'sort my life out' and 600 of 'sort my head out', showing the latter to be extremely rare.

What was even rarer was the co-occurrence of both phrases in one document, that is, sorting out one's life and one's head. Seventeen occurrences on Google makes the combination almost unique. The other interesting thing to note is the sequence: in the phone texts the earlier text refers to the *head* being sorted, the later text refers to *life* being sorted. This is the same sequence as in the interview: 'head sorted out . . . sorted her life out'. Thus, not only do we have the same two elements in the interview as in the (separate) texts, but they are in the same sequence.

Of course I was aware that we were dealing with differences between written[1] and spoken language, and that we were dealing with two mobile phone texts rather than one – but, even so, it seemed too much like coincidence. I reported back to the detectives leading the inquiry that in my view there was a high probability that Mr Simmerson was the author of the mobile phone messages. They concluded from this that the chances of Julie coming back were extremely remote. What had been a missing person inquiry soon became a murder investigation.

The search for Julie or her body now intensified. Officers spent hundreds of hours searching the countryside between Creswell and Sheffield, while a whole team was tasked with looking at CCTV videos of all the businesses in the area. They also contacted many of Mr Simmerson's friends and clients. An image which popped up repeatedly on CCTVs several days after Julie's disappearance was of a silver-coloured Ford Ranger being driven around with an oil drum on the back of the vehicle. Coincidentally, on the night Julie disappeared Simmerson had asked a client of his if he could bury an oil drum on his land – he claimed it contained several weapons which he did not want the police to know about. The client refused. At the same time as his affair with Julie, Simmerson had also started a relationship with another woman, in fact the 20-year old daughter of his client. As the oil drum sat on the back of his Ford Ranger, he seduced the girl in her father's barn. The oil drum was eventually traced to a scrapyard. Inside was the body of Julie Turner. She had been shot through the head.

Confronted with the fact of Julie being found in the barrel that he had had on the back of his Ford Ranger, Simmerson claimed that Julie had found the gun in his glove compartment and shot herself accidentally. However, he appeared to have forgotten the letter he had written only a few weeks before Julie's death, and seemed somewhat shocked when confronted with the references to guns and shooting, including the following:

> Julie am afraid doesn't seem concerned about the money prob. aprt from spending it. I love her dearly but I can see it coming to the final shot to finally be together. I am sane writing this and just waiting for the machine to carry this out.

> Mike, is taking his time to fetch this gun(?) and I am not sure which one to go for? either, hopefully are quick and easy.

Hence, Simmerson's request to purchase a gun from 'Mike' was already known to the detectives before they found the oil barrel, as well as his despair over his financial situation and the fact that he blamed Julie for it. For this reason, the officers did not believe that Julie had shot herself. The jury did not believe Simmerson either, and nor did any of Julie's family or friends. On 8 November 2005, less than 6 months after Julie's death, he was sentenced to life imprisonment at Sheffield Crown Court by Mr Justice Pitchers, who recommended a minimum term of 25 years. When he was sentenced Simmerson showed absolutely no remorse for Julie's death and no emotion at the sentence he received. The mobile telephone which had sent the texts was never recovered.

Note

1. It may be more accurate to refer to phone text language as a hybrid mode: it has properties of both written and spoken language.

2

THE BICYCLE MURDER

It was just 10 minutes past midnight on Friday, 5 May 2007 when Stephen Green left his place of work at Dunstable, in Bedfordshire on his bicycle. A single man of 50 years of age, Stephen, a former soldier, was popular in his community. He began making his way home and arrived at the Lewsey Bridge underpass near the M1. For those familiar with the area it runs between Buteley Road and Ravenhill Way in Luton. It was here that Mr Green was set upon by a gang of youths, robbed and left to die after being viciously kicked in the head.

Initially, there were no clues, but the bicycle was examined and a fingerprint was found on one of the tyres. This fingerprint led to a young man who, in turn, was known to be connected with several others with whom he regularly drank and took drugs. Their mobile phones were seized and it was noted that a number of texts had been sent between one of the phones and another phone at about the time of the robbery. The process of triangulation of signals was then applied and a mobile phone belonging to one Darryl Bennett was found to have been sending texts from the area of the crime at about the time the attack was thought to have taken place. However, by the time Bennett's phone was seized all of the texts had been deleted from it, and were only to be found on the phone of his girlfriend, Trish (not her real name), as incoming messages.

For some reason the time of receipt of incoming texts was not recorded on Trish's phone. So, although the time at which mobile phone texts were sent was recorded, there was no way of knowing when incoming texts were received. Hence, the sequence of the incoming texts could not be established automatically. In addition, it seemed that Trish had deleted some of the texts – perhaps not intentionally. The task for forensic linguistics was to see whether the texts could be placed in sequence – in other words, to attempt a reconstruction of the conversation from fragments. This was not helped by the texts being in a very local 'teenspeak' mobile phone dialect – in fact it was more like a group idiolect, a kind of slang that seems to have grown up around the core group of youths who were suspected of the attack, their friends and girlfriends, and even older family members. Nowadays, linguists refer to 'textspeak' when talking about the language used in mobile phone texts. However, there are many varieties of textspeak. It used to be thought, for example, that only younger users abbreviated their texts – for example '2u' for 'to you', '4got' for 'forgot' and so on – but an early text case disabused me of this notion. This concerned the murder of Peter Solheim in Cornwall in 2004. Texts were sent from a female acquaintance of his to his partner purporting to be from him as he was supposedly preparing for a trip in his boat to France. In the meantime, as the jury at Truro Crown Court found in July 2006, she had been conspiring to murder him. What was noticeable about Margaret James' texts was their almost excessive use of abbreviation, which was in stark contrast to Mr Solheim's texts. I mention this merely to point out that it would be a mistake to assume that only young people abbreviate their texts.

To return to the present case, the main participants in the mobile phone text conversation were Darryl and Trish, although there were also texts from others. In all, there were over 150 texts to translate and sequence. My starting hypothesis, which I would have to test thoroughly, was that Trish and Darryl Bennett were engaged in a text conversation in which an assault and robbery were mentioned. Having translated all of the texts, I then had to use linguistic knowledge of how conversations are structured to see whether the different fragments were able to fit together. In some respects mobile phone text conversations are very similar to spoken conversations. Later on I received the service provider's billing log which was helpful in putting the final pieces of the puzzle together. The billing logs do not contain the actual SMS texts, but they contain times and dates and can give an indication of the length of a text.

Because the texts were heavily abbreviated, the officers working on the case were only able to understand some of them. A small number of them were quite undecipherable in the beginning, and required considerable research of 'teenspeak' on the internet and from other sources. Of the 152 texts to be analysed, 60 were sent from Trish to Bennett and 41 were from Bennett to Trish. Other texts in the time period following the incident include those sent from Trish to her aunt, and to her cousin Shane Liddy, one of the suspects. Trish also sent texts to a friend, Cecilia (not her real name). There were also several texts sent to someone I will call 'Max'.

The textspeak used in the present case appeared to include aspects of chat room conversations where the interaction between participants is sometimes very rapid, necessitating a terse, abbreviated form of language.

An unpleasant component of the texts in the present case was the quantity and variety of derogatory terms traded between interactants, including 'beuch' (bitch), 'niger' (nigger) or 'af' (African), 'white', 'slut', and so on. Strangely, there did not appear to be any racist or sexist motivation in the trading of these epithets. As curious as it might sound, they seemed almost like terms of endearment. I apologise if these terms offend readers: they are not meant to – I am merely reporting what I found.

It should be stressed that no act of interpreting or translating can be described as 'exact' or 'precise'. This applies to translating between any two languages as much as it does to the translation of textspeak into standard English. One of the key problems in translating occurs when the context is not understood or not given. We little realize how much we rely on the circumstances of a particular situation to understand what people are saying to us or to each other. This is why fragments of overheard conversations are often difficult to decode, when we do not know the participants. In fact the misinterpreting of a remark that was intended to be innocent can come as a shock to us. This usually happens because someone we do not know overhears something we say, but without being aware of the background to our conversation. Such incidents frequently result in all kinds of misunderstandings between people. In the present case there were many examples of this. For example, one of the texts received from Darryl was this one (the original is given on the left, with the translation on the right):

Darryl Bennett: U joka dat film froze 10 minz ago	**Darryl Bennett**: You joker (or: you're joking). That film froze 10 minutes ago.

Another example from Darryl's phone was 'Must of boy i cant remeba shit'. The problem was to discover where these messages fitted into the context of the ongoing conversation between Darryl and Trish, a conversation that spanned a night, a day and another night. Looking at the above example, it is evident that Trish must have first referred to a film. This then became 'that film'. This process of connecting messages using words such as 'this', 'that', and so on is known as cohesion – which I have referred to elsewhere as a kind of 'textual glue' between sentences. In the second example 'Must of boy i cant remeba shit', 'must of' is clearly substituting for a full verb, and one which is related to being unable to remember something. Hence, the possibilities range around such activities as drinking excessively, being high on drugs or even just falling asleep.

In assessing whether a text was a candidate for inclusion at a particular point, I looked for a number of other indicators in addition to those mentioned above, such as an apparently straightforward answer to a question – for example 'Yes', 'I did', 'he isn't', and so on. What linguists call 'finite elements' are useful in this regard – by which I mean the subject of the sentence, for example, 'he', 'I', 'she' and so on, and the verb following the subject, for instance 'do', 'did', 'have', and so on. What we have to realize though is that the text conversation is not necessarily the complete conversation between the participants. These people might be phoning each other in between texting and they could also be speaking to each other face to face. What was evident from this case was that sometimes the suspects were texting each other even when they were in the same house. Here is an early text in the sequence (translated):

Nick, Bessie saw the blood on your hands. Darryl, Bessie said she saw the cut on your head. You said you wouldn't do a robbery again, and you promised you wouldn't do anything when Shane was there. You lied trish x

This text was sent about half an hour after the robbery. Darryl's reply appears to have been simply: 'Wat we didnt Trish'. Using a knowledge of cohesion I was able to say that the likely next text to Darryl was this one:

Why are you lying. Shane told me. You're an idiot. You promised you wouldn't. Now I know who I can and can't trust, and you're on the can't trust list x

Hence, in the above sequence, Trish – after telling Nick that Bessie saw *the* blood on his hands, then appears to be accusing Darryl of having broken a promise by having been involved in a robbery, and of having had Shane with him at the time. There was an earlier text from Trish to Nick asking him to get Shane to hurry up. Evidently, Trish now has reason to believe that Shane was with Darryl, rather than with Nick, and that Bennett committed a robbery. She then goes on '. . . what were you going to say? You said "first things first . . ." then you stopped. What was that all about?' Here she seems to be seeking clarification about something that Bennett, apparently began to say, namely 'First things first'. Later we learn, from another text, that some time before sending this text Trish was at the Lewsey tunnel where she and Bennett, according to that text, had been having a conversation. It thus seems that we are able to place Trish at or near the scene of the crime shortly after it had been committed.

This, plus the structure of the above message indicates that she probably did not witness the attack – if she had done so she would probably not have said that Bessie had seen the cut on his head, but that she had actually witnessed the attack. Notice that Trish says 'saw *the* blood on your hands . . . *the* cut on your head' as opposed to 'saw blood on your hands . . . *a* cut on your head'. This implies that both the blood and the cut are given elements of their conversation. In other words, it is possible that Trish herself has seen these, but that she is using Bessie's reference to these observations in order perhaps to give them more weight. Alternatively, it is possible that they had already been referred to when the couple were conversing at the bridge.

So, what we have had so far is an accusation by Trish, a denial by Darryl, and a further accusation by Trish. It is logical, therefore to assume, that a further denial by Darryl is inevitable, and indeed that is exactly what happens, because we have a text: 'Shane chattin shit, trust me', which I believe was the next text in the sequence. We next have a text sent by Trish to her friend 'Max'. In addition to other matters mentioned, the text ends with the following reference to her earlier conversation with Darryl: 'Darryl txtn me bulshit. He pissin me off. He broke a promise'. This 'promise' appears to relate to her earlier accusation that Darryl had broken a promise by committing a robbery and taking Shane, a younger boy, with him. This text was known to have been sent from Trish's phone at 1.13 a.m. The importance of this text to Max is twofold: first, it appears to confirm the reconstructed exchange between Bennett and Trish which I have given above and, secondly, we can apparently date and time it with complete accuracy.

We have another text exchange between Trish and Bennett, in which she asks him what he was going to say at the Lewsey tunnel: 'What were you going to say last night near Lewsey Bridge? You pulled me back and told Shane and that to walk on and you said "right, first things first" and then you stopped. What were you going to say if you can remember? X'. I suggest that this text was sent on the day following her seeing Darryl at the tunnel with blood on his hands, because it specifically states 'last night', mentions 'Lewsey Bridge' and there is also a reference to Shane having been there.

We have a text from Darryl in which he says 'Fuck knowz most probaly gona chat shit'. This appears to be a reply to something, and I suggest it is a reply to the previous text, because it contains two of the elements from that text, namely that he was *about* to do something 'probaly gona' (*trans*: probably going to) and that that something was to 'chat shit' (*trans*: talk rubbish). The above text also seems to relate to the events of 5 May 2007, in that it implies that the recipient, whom we know to be Darryl Bennett, has done something he said he would not do – namely assault people and rob them. This is similar to Trish's other claims that Bennett has broken a promise to her, namely, that 'you said you wouldn't do robbery again'. There is a reference also to Darryl 'going down' soon, that is, going to prison – believed to be in relation to a previous offence.

As part of my analysis I considered alternative explanations for the texts and I also experimented with other sequences of the text conversations. I was unable to come up with any explanation which would indicate that Trish was not referring to a real robbery and assault. In support of this we see her apparent disappointment at what she claims is Darryl's broken promise, her reference to what Bessie saw, her mention of her disappointment to 'Max' and her later, repeated, accusation that he, Darryl, had broken his word.

Of course it is impossible to be sure that one has reconstructed a text conversation with total accuracy. It is not an exact science. Nevertheless, I was unable to find a viable alternative sequence of texts between Darryl and Trish and the other participants. I believe all of the suspects had plenty of opportunities to refute my analysis and to come up with their own explanations. One point on which I sought confirmation from the officers related to the actual authorship of the texts. Although the texts were on Darryl and Trish's phones, it was nevertheless important to establish that they had not allowed others to text at that time. Although I did not receive confirmation of this point, it was never refuted that each of them had done their own texting.

Following my analysis and reconstruction of the text message conversations these were submitted to the court and, having initially denied the offence, three of the youths decided to own up to their part in the crime. They initially pleaded guilty to manslaughter but the jury found all four guilty of murder. They were sentenced to life imprisonment at Luton Crown Court in May 2008.

3

HEROIN SMUGGLING INTO A PRISON

One afternoon in March some years ago I received a phone call from a detective in the Midlands. She asked me to examine a number of audio recordings relating to an attempted smuggling of heroin into a prison. I was asked to compare the voice of an unknown female with the voice of one Sheila de Vere and the voice of an unknown male with that of one Dwayne Hillingdon, then an almost permanent subscriber to Her Majesty's Prison plan. The detective told me that there was also some 'interesting' conversation on the tapes which she would like me to comment on.

I awaited the arrival of the inquiry documents with interest. When the documents arrived, the case turned out to be even more intriguing than I had expected. An envelope had arrived at a prison addressed to Dwayne Hillingdon. Although it bore the correct code associated with a certain kind of privileged communication prisoners are sometimes entitled to receive, its bulky nature caused it to be viewed suspiciously by the authorities and it was opened. It was found to contain a large amount of high grade heroin, secreted within plastic bags. As part of the police inquiry into the matter telephone calls made by Hillingdon were accessed. A number of these calls were to a female and appeared to refer to a particular type of envelope being sent into the prison. Hillingdon's interlocutor in these calls was said to be Sheila de Vere. The detective claimed she had been assisting him in his little smuggling endeavour.

There were two separate inquiries. First, I had to find out whether the female voice was likely to be that of Sheila de Vere and whether the male voice was likely to be that of Dwayne Hillingdon, both voices by comparison with police interview tapes. The second thing I had to figure out was whether the male and female speakers, alleged to be Dwayne and Sheila, were in fact discussing sending heroin into prison, concealed within an envelope, or whether they were talking about some other, harmless matter.

I listened to the tapes of the telephone calls and of the police interview with Sheila de Vere and realized that the voices sounded quite different from each other – at least on first impressions. In interviews with the police, the female sounded very breathy. Like someone who had been running and wanted to charm you at the same time. Sometimes, however, her voice broke out into a kind of creakiness, as though she had a frog in her throat. On the other hand, the female voice on the phone sounded quite different, very chatty and friendly, much louder than the voice in the interviews.

However, close listening showed that there were similarities. Just occasionally the woman on the phone got a little breathy, and then sometimes went a bit creaky too. Both voices also had a peculiar way of stressing words. Phoneticians talk about a tone group – a group of words in a phrase or clause which sounds like one 'packet' of information. Some people call them information units or chunks. Within any tone group a certain number of syllables will be stressed. You can stress a syllable in a number of ways: you can lengthen it, or you can raise or lower its pitch, or you can alter length and pitch together. What Sheila did was to take the last syllable of the tone group and then both raise and lengthen it. This was perhaps not exceptional, but then she did something more – she added creaky voice to the concoction. Both tapes showed evidence of this. It took about 4 hours of listening to figure out what was happening. She also did something else. She would take a long word like 'relationship' and lengthen the stressed syllable and turn it into – effectively – three syllables, like this: 'rela-ay-iy-tionship'. When you get three syllables for the price of one it's called a triphthong. Sheila did this all the time in the interview and also on the phone. For instance, at one point she's disputing with the detectives that she and Dwayne are that close: 'It's not a real rela-ay-iy-tionship' she protests. Of course there is a dialect element to this: a lot of people from certain parts of the Midlands do things like this too.

Finally, I listened to her voice to try to discover what pitch it mostly worked at. This is a thing known as fundamental frequency. Fundamental frequency is a strange thing. This is how it works. When we hear a voice saying a single sound (called a phoneme), like 'aah' we think we are hearing just one sound, but we are not. We are hearing the sound plus the harmonics of the sound. When you put the voice on the spectrogram you see the harmonics – but you do not see the fundamental sound. You have to calculate it, or use a program to derive it in some way. People tend to have a distinctive fundamental frequency to their voice. It is to do with the size and shape of the vocal tract – loosely described as the inside of the mouth down to the vocal cords, plus the shape of the lips, plus the nasal tract. People with differently shaped vocal tracts are likely to have different fundamental frequencies. Of course there are overlaps between people, and nobody is absolutely constant in the delivery of the

fundamental frequency. Even so, you get some idea of the distinctive-
ness of a person's voice from this measure. Sheila's voice and the voice
on the phone had very similar fundamental frequencies. Based on all of
this I concluded that the two voices belonged to one individual. I use a
scale of judgements for this kind of assessment – it enables me to state
the degree of likelihood of an observation.

The next task was to listen to the male's voice. He, Dwayne, was interviewed in a prison interview room. This happens when the prisoner is
judged too much of a security risk to move to a police station for interview.
Dwayne was a dangerous man. Several of his acquaintances had turned up
in car parks dead or nearly dead. Several others had disappeared. As the
detective dryly explained to me: 'You would not want to live next door
to Dwayne'. Because they could not safely transport Dwayne to a police
station they interviewed him in the prison interview room. The only
trouble is that prisons are noisy places, even supposedly quiet areas like
interview rooms. The officers who were conducting the interview were so
fixated on talking to Dwayne that they probably did not pick up all the
background noise. So, what I had to do was to compare Dwayne's prison
interview room voice with the voice on the phone. Dwayne was adamant
that it was not him. Somebody must have gone into his cell and stolen his
phone card with his PIN on it. He had been bullied, he said, when he first
came to the prison. Of course he had not reported either the bullying or
the theft because 'things don't work like that in prison'. The officers who
interviewed him had some difficulty believing this story. Dwayne is about
6 feet 4 inches tall and is built like a Greek god with more biceps than
most, not to mention what they described as a rather mean countenance
(unlike Greek gods). Hence, this seemed to be something of a fabrication
on Dwayne's part – either that or a reckless regard on the part of other
prisoners for their own safety.

Aside from being in a noisy environment, another problem with the
prison interview room was that the microphone seemed to have been
placed about 10 yards away from where Dwayne was sitting. Maybe they
were afraid he would steal it or rip it out or something. The officers
were audible and clear, but the prisoner was not, even though at times
he got quite angry at their questions. Dwayne is not a man who likes to
be asked anything, as several of his previous best friends had testified.
In the end I had to admit that I was only relatively certain of the identification. I gave it a 3 out of 5, whereas with Sheila I had been confident
that it was a 4 out of 5.

The conversation between the loving couple on the phone was curious. Everything the male says seems to have been spoken out of the side
of the mouth, just like you see in the movies. Everything is in code, but

not the usual prisoner's code: thus £150 is 'one and a half', a postage stamp is a 'sticky'.

It takes the male about 10 minutes to get to the fact that the female has to send him an envelope disguised in a certain way. The male is doing his best to avoid being too explicit. To this end at one point he spells out the word 'envelope'. The trouble is the male and spelling do not quite see to eye, so we get 'e–m–v–i–l–i–p', 'l–e–n–v–e–l–o–p' and so forth, none of which mean a thing to the long-suffering female who, if the couple were not engaged in a highly criminal enterprise, would surely deserve a reward for patience. Finally, the female spells out 'envelope' quite correctly and the male agrees, that this is what it is. At this point he actually says the word 'envelope' which meant that both the female and myself had suffered for 10 minutes in vain. They then refer to the code that is to be placed on the envelope, but – again – the male is trying to avoid being too precise:

M: You know your phone number?
F: Yeah, course I do.
M: Well you know the last number in it . . .
F: My last phone number?
M: No, not your last number, listen to me –
F: Yeah, I'm listening.
M: I mean if you took your phone number, yeah, and looked at the last number in it.
F: Oh yeah, you mean like the last number in my number?
M: Yeah.
F: It's a four.
M: What?
F: Four, it's a four –
M: No, don't say it – I don't want anyone to hear it.
F: Oh, okay, I won't say it then. . . .

and so on and so forth.

The other amusing part of the conversation related to the heroin, and how it was to be presented in the envelope. The male tells the female that she's got to take 'the stuff' home and mash it 'on the kitchen table'. Before this, however, she has to make contact with the dope peddler, and persuade him to deal with her.

F: He doesn't like coming out in the day time.
M: Oh, one of those?

F: Yeah, he's one of those. Last time I had to wait until nearly midnight cause he said it was too dodgy. He's got form.

M: He's got what?

F: Form, you know – he says he's been stitched by the old bill in the past.

M: Oh, yeah, those bastards, I know what that's like.

F: Yeah, then what do I do?

M: Well, you get it home and mash it up, and then put it in bags in the en– the you know whatsitsname.

In the end, however, despite their best efforts to avoid being transparent, nothing was more transparent than their conversation. They had quite obviously conspired to smuggle an envelope into prison under the guise of a privileged communication. The envelope, however, had been packed so badly, that its bulky appearance had caught the attention of the prison staff. In the meantime, Dwayne had actually sold all of the heroin to his fellow inmates and had received their money and, in fact, had spent it. I imagine his popularity ratings amongst his colleagues must have taken a sudden nosedive.

Finally, in court, faced with what the police officers described as overwhelming linguistic and phonetic evidence, both Dwayne and Sheila were found guilty of conspiring to smuggle heroin into a prison. Dwayne had 4 years added to his original sentence and Sheila was sentenced to 2 years in custody. What was interesting about this case was that it was a combination of linguistic and phonetic evidence. In fact, in my experience, it is rare for voice identification cases not to include at least some aspects of linguistics.

4

IS *THE DA VINCI CODE* PLAGIARISM?

In 2004 the world was hit by a publishing phenomenon encapsulated in the intriguing title, 'The Da Vinci Code'. Within months of coming off the presses, *The Da Vinci Code* was a publishing phenomenon. It was a physical presence in every bookshop in the United Kingdom and the United States of America, and was translated into scores of languages from French to Japanese. A photograph of the writer, a New Englander by the name of Dan Brown, stared out from dustjackets and newspaper articles from Sydney to Cape Town, from Zagreb to Madrid to New York. In time the book spawned a succession of other products, such as the Da Vinci Code notebook, the Da Vinci Code pen and pencil set, t-shirts, DVDs, drinks coasters and so on. A single book had become a successful franchise. I believe there was a Da Vinci Code theme tune in the charts, and even Da Vinci Code bus tours of Paris and a certain ancient parish church in Scotland.

It was rare to meet anyone who had not read *The Da Vinci Code*. Imagine my surprise, therefore, when I got a phone call from Lew Perdue, an author based in California, claiming that *The Da Vinci Code* (hereafter *DVC*) had been plagiarized from his own works, mostly from Perdue's *Daughter of God* (2000 – hereafter *DoG*) and *The Da Vinci Legacy* (1983 – hereafter *Legacy*), as well as from another early work, *The Linz Testament* (1985 – hereafter *Linz*). All of Perdue's works were published long before the Da Vinci Code.

According to Perdue, each of his novels built on its predecessor. In *Legacy* Perdue began by exploring the topic of Leonardo da Vinci and religion in a thriller format, but later felt that this theme should be added to that of exploring the notion of 'the lost feminine' in modern-day religions. Perdue claims that the later books are not mere reworkings of the earlier ones, but major developments, not only in terms of characterization and plot but also in terms of the underlying infrastructure of facts and knowledge, although there are still many points of similarity between the earlier and later books.

The central concern with both Brown and Perdue's novels is the threat to the Roman Catholic Church posed by the existence of a set of secret documents. In each novel there are powerful forces lined up on either side of a single question: to keep the documents secret or to expose them to the world? Keeping them secret would ensure the continuation of the Church's power, whereas exposure would considerably weaken the Church's authority. The novels contain a potent cocktail of romance, murder, ecclesiastical corruption, myth and high art. While some of these components are only to be expected in thriller novels, the reader is invited to consider whether Brown, in producing *DVC* exceeded the generic and actually plagiarized from Perdue. Although I was engaged by Lew Perdue, I will not give my own opinion in this chapter beyond recording the observations I made at the time. I leave it to the reader to solve the question of whether any plagiarism by Brown took place or not. To help the reader in this quest I need to point out the distinction between **plagiarism** on the one hand and **copyright infringement** on the other.

Plagiarism is the unacknowledged use of material authored by someone else, either by taking the precise phrasing of that individual or by rephrasing their ideas. Plagiarism is essentially an academic offence. Universities and schools can impose severe penalties on those who plagiarise, but the ultimate intention is not punition itself but the encouragement of reflection, self-expression and the development of one's own ideas. There are three main kinds of plagiarism: literal plagiarism, mosaic plagiarism and conceptual plagiarism. Literal plagiarism is the use of the exact words of someone else, mosaic plagiarism is the re-arrangement of another's words and phrases, often interspersed with the plagiarist's own language. The hope in mosaic plagiarism is to avoid detection, but there are all sorts of ways of detecting both literal and mosaic plagiarism. Conceptual plagiarism is harder to detect, but a reader familiar with the source material will usually detect the theft. Note that for plagiarism to exist the material used must be unacknowledged or not acknowledged properly, or used to excess. In other words, the plagiarist claims to be the originator of the material, or does not fully or properly acknowledge the source of the material, or relies too heavily on it.

Copyright infringement on the other hand is generally a civil matter: it is not a crime. People who have infringed someone else's copyright do not usually get a criminal record, though they may have to pay damages. It is also the copying of material, in the precise ways mentioned above, also without proper acknowledgement, but as suggested by the term, the copyright of the source author has been infringed. The copyist has taken someone else's material, published it and then claimed to own the copyright on it. Hence, copyright infringement is a species of plagiarism, but it is the fact that it has specific legal implications that makes us call it 'copyright infringement' rather than 'plagiarism'. It is the same physical activity, but one which is carried out in a different social framework.

It is not just a question of similarities between works that causes infringement to take place, but the extent, type and relative significance of *protectible* similarities across the two works. An historical fact is not a protectible similarity, nor is a title, nor is an idea. Many small plot similarities are not protectible either. A concept becomes protectible when it depends on its expression within the context of the work. If what amounts to a unique expression of a concept, character or idea, is copied then the work has been infringed because that in it which was protectible has been violated. Copyright infringement can also be said to have taken place if the extent of the copying is excessive, and would include substantial plot lines, character similarities and even narrative sequence.

Therefore, in considering the points made in the following sections, the reader is really being asked to judge to what extent – if any – Brown has violated individual, unique or highly unusual expressions of key concepts within Perdue's books. The reader who has read the novels first would be in a better position to decide the issue of infringement, but hopefully you will find the account below sufficient to reach a decision for yourself. I will try to explain the contexts to assist you to do this.

Overall Structure of the Novels

Several plot lines run through the novels. One set of examples concerns the way in which the hero becomes involved in the quest to locate the documents which contain the secrets, said to be so dangerous and 'explosive' that members of various religious sects are prepared to kill to conceal them.

This theme of 'explosive secrets' is common to both Perdue and Brown and a quest to find them is launched – in each case – when a renowned international expert is murdered by a member of a religious sect. In each book the expert is the fourth person within his area of expertise to be killed in this way (not the second, third or fifth, but in each case, the fourth). As it happens the hero and the expert in each author's work are actually acquainted with each other. The murdered expert in each author's work writes a last message in his own blood, and – finally – the hero, in each author's work, is accused of the murder of the expert. More details are shown in the graph in Figure 4.1, where each bar relates to the page number in the respective book where the relevant detail is

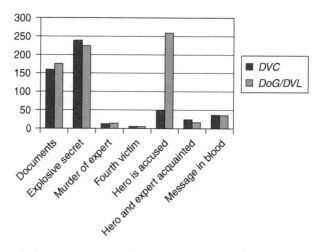

Figure 4.1. Graph showing similarities across Brown and Perdue

mentioned. As the reader will observe, there are seven plot features – which I believe to be representative of the similarities across the books in general – mentioned in the description above, and shown in the graph in Figure 4.1 – six of these seven plot features are in sequence and on very similar page numbers within their respective books.

So, for example, the existence of the secret documents is first aired on Page 158 in *DVC*, and Page 175 in *DoG/DVL*. The 'explosive' secret these documents contain is first aired on Page 239 in *DVC* and Page 226 in *DoG*. The expert – whose murder launches the quest to find the documents is murdered on Page 11 in *DVC* and 15 in *DoG*. The fact that the hero and expert are acquainted is mentioned on Page 22 and Page 15 respectively. And the fact that the dying expert wrote a message in his own blood, is mentioned – in both books – exactly on Page 35. The only difference as far as sequence in the above plot line is concerned, relates to when the hero is accused of having murdered the expert. In *DVC* it happens early, Page 47, while in *DoG* it happens later, on Page 260. So we have seven somewhat similar plot features out of seven across both Brown and Perdue, of which six are in sequence. To put the above in the context of our inquiry, are these elements protectible? Before making up our minds, let us continue with other similarities, beginning with the portrayal of the hero and heroine in each work.

First, let us consider the heroes. They are of a similar age, their looks seem similar, and they appear to have a similar range of personal anxieties and difficulties. Thus, both are professors of religion in their late thirties to early forties, with a particular interest in the Emperor Constantine and female deities and both are Leonardo specialists. Perhaps, given that such books are intended to appeal to a mass audience the age group is fairly predictable and, given also that the theme of the books is religious it is not surprising that they should both be professors of religion. However, the reader might consider that the parallels between their academic interests could be a little too similar. It may also be of some interest that both heroes have mild claustrophobia and are 'between relationships'. The latter point, however, is what gives many novels their romantic interest, and this is therefore an opportune moment to consider the heroines of the two novels. Interestingly, both heroines have similar coloured hair and eyes and do not conform to the standard heroine stereotype of 'slim', 'blonde', 'attractive' and so on.

The heroines have similar childhoods. They were each raised by a male figure after a family tragedy, and there are parallels in their education and careers. They both grew up in two countries and hence are fluent in two languages, they have interests in religion and art, are experts in cryptography and forgery, and both have worked for law enforcement agencies. Their names have similar associations with figures from religion, female deities and the Gnostic Gospels. Like the two heroes, the heroines of the two authors have many striking similarities and many identical points. In DoG Zoe's hair colour is not specified, but her predecessor in Linz had auburn hair: in DVC Sophie Neveu's hair is 'burgundy'. Sophie, like Zoe's predecessor has 'flashing green' eyes. Both women are either 'ample' of figure, or 'robust': they are not the typical slim heroines found in many books and films. The heroines are in the same age group, late twenties to early thirties – this latter point, however, is entirely predictable.

In DoG the heroine is Zoe Ridgeway who is an art broker whose expertise includes forgery detection and whose major interest is religion, whereas in DVC we have Sophie Neveu, a Paris police officer part of whose job is cryptography. She, like Zoe, has a major interest in religion and, also like Zoe, expertise in art. It should be noted that Perdue's earlier book DVL has the art journalist Suzanne Storm, who in fact is an undercover CIA agent. Are these points similar or just coincidental?

The origin of Perdue's Zoe Ridgeway is given by Perdue in DoG as the goddess Sophia of the Gnostic Gospels. In fact, the actual daughter of the Sophia of the Gnostic Gospels was called Zoe. Therefore, Perdue's heroine is symbolically the daughter of Sophia.

Brown's heroine, Sophie Neveu, is said to be a descendant of Mary Magdalene, the alleged wife of Jesus Christ. Mary Magdalene, in the

Gnostic Gospels (also the source for much of Brown's research) is actually a stand-in for the Sophia of the Gnostic Gospels, according to well-known writer Margaret Starbird (whom Brown admits to having consulted). In other words, Brown's heroine is the lineal (rather than the symbolic) daughter of Sophia.

In both Perdue's and Brown's books, the goddess Sophia has been wronged by the church authorities who have deprived the goddess of her rightful position as an official deity in the church. The quest is to obtain access to the 'explosive' (both authors) documents which prove the link between Christ and the female goddess in each case, and thus demonstrate the inviolable position of the female deity in the church, and re-assert the 'sacred feminine' as the core of religion.

Shortly, we will consider the ways in which the secret documents are hidden, by whom and how they come to light, but for the moment it is worth pointing out an interesting parallel, in fact an error, found in both works.

There is a work called the *Codex Leicester*, an actual book written by the Renaissance scientist and artist, Leonardo da Vinci. *The Codex Leicester* is written on linen paper, but Perdue erroneously records this as 'parchment' in his book – an error which extensive researches (across the internet, as well as other sources) did not uncover as occurring elsewhere. In his book Brown repeats this error. As you are reaching the decision on copyright infringement for yourself, I would invite you at this point to consider the implications of this. The point is, to my knowledge, no other mention of *The Codex Leicester* is on 'parchment' anywhere else other than in these two authors' books. The repetition of errors across two authors is often considered by courts to be indicative of copyright infringement. What is your view?

The documents referred to earlier contain information which is so 'explosive' that, across both authors, it could have devastating consequences for the future of the Catholic Church. For this reason, as regular readers of thrillers will appreciate, there is a complex web of narrative material surrounding the announcement of the documents, the quest for their location and their final uncovering.

In Perdue's *DoG* there is a golden key which is hidden in a painting (*The Home of the Lady of Our Redeemer*). This golden key (accompanied by a gold ingot with the account number) allows access to a safe deposit box in a Zurich bank. The key does not actually open a lock as such.

In Brown's *DVC* there is also a golden key, which is hidden – not *in*, in this case, but *behind* – a painting (*Madonna of the Rocks*). This is a laser-cut gold key also allowing access to a safe deposit box in a Zurich-related bank. Just as in Perdue's case, Brown's key doesn't actually turn an actual lock either. Interestingly, both paintings in both sets of novels are painted on wood (in general – but not always – this tends to tie paintings to particular periods and particular regions, because wood was mostly supplanted as a painting ground by canvas).

In *DVC* Sophie finds the key hidden behind the painting while she and Langdon are in the Louvre. The reader will know that at the beginning of the novel we have the Louvre curator being murdered by a member of a secret brotherhood.

This dying curator leaves a written message, which he writes on the glass that covers the *Mona Lisa*. This message tells Sophie where to locate the key which, as mentioned above, is concealed in the same room, secreted behind the painting *Madonna of the Rocks*. The curator was actually Sophie's grandfather.

In *DoG* there is also a triple connection between the painting, the heroine and the curator: *DoG*'s Zoe, the heroine is sent the painting (which contains the key) by Max (the curator) who, as it happens is also killed by a member of a secret order.

In *DVC* Sophie finds the key and is baffled by it, because she has no instructions about what she is to do with the key, mainly because it does not look like a 'normal' key, but rather a kind of cypher. The key in *DVC* is made of gold and contains a series of laser-cut pits and reliefs. It is also designed to be read by a laser. It first allows Sophie access to enter the car park and then the building of the bank. Previously I described this as a 'Zurich related' bank. What I meant by this is that the bank is in fact the Zurich Bank of Commerce in Paris. Unlike *DoG*, the bank is not located in Zurich. Finally, in *DVC*, the key controls a computer-operated device which gives the protagonists access to the safe deposit box which contain the documents – the details of which I will explain below.

In *DoG*, Zoe – as mentioned above – is sent the painting. She and Seth go to the person who owned the shop where the painting was framed and in the course of this conversation, they learn that if they take the painting to a particular bank in Zurich they will have access to an important safe deposit box (as mentioned before, the key is embedded in the painting). (Perdue's painting is by a real artist but is not a real painting – the title plays on the iconic value of the words 'lady' and 'redeemer'.)

In Brown's book the reference is to an actual painter, Leonardo, who painted two versions of *Madonna of the Rocks* on wood, one of which is in the National Gallery, London, with the other in the Louvre.

Perdue's key requires removal, along with the gold ingot, from the painting. The gold ingot contains the account number and is also used as a counter balance to open the vault which contains a box which in turn has to be decoded in order to reveal the secret documents.

In Brown's case the pitted reliefs and impressions of the golden key actuate a somewhat intricate technological device, which delivers a safe deposit box. This in turn contains a box which holds a carved wooden puzzle where the dials have to be set to the correct combination for the puzzle to open.

In Perdue's case the safe deposit box contains a briefcase with a combination which also has to be set properly. The key point is that each narrative utilizes a key which is not a conventional key to open a safe deposit box which contains another container which has to be decoded to reveal a secret, which, as it happens, relates to the actual divine nature of the female goddess as an integral deity of the Church which the Church in turn has attempted, through a secret brotherhood, to suppress, partly through murdering – in each case, the curator of a museum.

What is inside the containers found in the safe deposit boxes is information that sends the protagonists in each of the novels on the next leg of their quest. In both cases this is to another country. In Brown they are taken from Paris to London, while in Perdue the protagonists are taken from Zurich to Salzburg.

In both cases the ultimate documents are supposed to be at the destination. In Perdue's case the hero and heroine get to the documents, but in Brown there is another red herring. In Brown's case the documents are not found, but in Perdue's the documents are destroyed.

At this stage the reader may wish to consider whether what I have described above sounds like plagiarism. I should state that what has come so far has nothing to do with linguistics – and this is true of most academic inquiries into plagiarism. All I have done so far is to simply look at literal and conceptual similarities between two works. I will now move into the arena of linguistics, and with it will come a range of exotic terms. I will try to keep them to a minimum.

The first term I will introduce is the idea of the *frame*. This is an important concept.

For linguists the frame is part of how humans think. We base our verbal behaviour on frames. Frames contain the elements of a typical interaction between two (or more) people. Thus, when you go to a fast food restaurant and order a burger and fries to take away you would expect certain things to happen, and you would expect them to happen in a certain order. For example, typically, you would queue up and wait to be served. Once you had the attention of the person serving they would then probably ask you what you want. You would specify. They would ask you whether you want, large, medium or regular. Again, you would specify if you had not already done so. They would go away, prepare your package, bag it and ask for payment. You would pay. They will give you your change and thank you. You thank them and say good-bye. It is linguistically very predictable – hence the term 'frame', a structure consisting of a support (the fast food restaurant) and certain ubiquitous 'bolt on' elements – the serving process, the requests, confirmations, greetings and so on.

You would not expect the person serving to suddenly start insulting you, or to ask you whether your parents were still alive. Similarly, that individual would not expect you to ask for a car to hire or an insurance policy: these elements are simply not in the appropriate cognitive frame for going to a fast food restaurant and ordering a take away.

What happens in the Perdue-Brown case is that in some instances Brown borrows Perdue's frames and modifies them. I believe he does this by adapting surface features, taking simple elements from the host frame and then elaborating them. I will now give an example.

In Perdue's *DoG*, the hero and heroine at one point have to enter a Swiss bank to retrieve the contents of a safe deposit box. Their mission is to discover the documents that the Church has been anxious to keep secret. In Brown's *DVC*, the hero and heroine also have to enter a bank where they also have to access a safe deposit box. They do not know what is in the safe deposit box, but it also turns out to be an important church document, revealing secrets which are potentially embarrassing to the Church. In the following two excerpts we can see how the two authors describe the moment when, in both books, the hero and heroine are shown into what is called, in both books, the *viewing room*. At the moment of entering, in each novel, neither Perdue's characters nor Brown's characters know either that they require a combination or what that combination is in order to access the safe deposit boxes. This information materializes during the course of their visit to the bank.

Perdue:
Ridgeway and Zoe looked silently about them. The room was the size of a luxury hotel room and furnished in much the same way. Besides the sofa and chairs, there was a television set, a rack of current magazines, a small computer terminal displaying financial quotes, and a wet bar stocked with liquor. Ridgeway went to the

wet bar, set the wrapped painting down on the counter, and filled a tumbler with water from a chilled bottle of Perrier.

Brown:
Langdon and Sophie stepped into another world. The small room before them looked like a lavish sitting room at a fine hotel. Gone were the metal and rivets, replaced with oriental carpets, dark oak furniture, and cushioned chairs. On the broad desk in the middle of the room, two crystal glasses sat beside an opened bottle of Perrier, its bubbles still fizzing. A pewter pot of coffee steamed beside it.

As can be seen, the two excerpts describe similar scenes. We need to ask ourselves two questions with regard to these frames:

1. Is there a common cognitive frame underlying both authors' descriptions?
2. If there is a common frame can we assume that the scene being described is just generic, and therefore the issue of plagiarism does not arise?

Like most people I have never personally been to a Swiss bank. Therefore I do not have a personal experiential frame which relates to that type of institution. I imagine that neither of these authors had ever been to one either. Therefore – assuming for the moment that the second piece had been written independently of the first – each author would have had to create the scene from scratch or, rather, would have adapted the scene from an existing frame. What would be their source? They may have seen a film which showed the inside of a Swiss bank, they may have read about Swiss banks, they may have seen photographs of one in a magazine. Even assuming none of the above was their source, we can say that most people in the richer countries probably have a concept of what a Swiss deposit bank is like, that it is something usually frequented only by rich people, and that it probably has something of an air of opulence about it. In all probability, therefore, we may say that there is a cognitive frame of some kind in many people's minds relating to the notion of 'Swiss deposit bank'. From this it would seem safe to develop the argument that each author arrived at his description based on this common non-personal frame. Or can we?

Before answering that question we need to consider an interesting aspect of plagiarism. When a writer copies the words of another writer, the copy needs to be disguised. This means that the copyist cannot use the same lexicon as the source, but has to adapt words and phrases found in the original. What happens linguistically at this stage is very interesting. We mostly make our vocabulary selections without thought. Words pop into our heads at a furious rate and we write them down or speak them without having to think too hard. However, the plagiarist does not have this luxury. The plagiarist has to avoid the very words which come most naturally and which, probably, are already in the text being copied. The plagiarist, therefore, has to adapt the vocabulary part of the cognitive frame – effectively twisting it slightly out of shape, in order to make the disguise complete. The result, very often, is that the plagiarist's vocabulary choices are to a greater or lesser extent, less than ideal. What this boils down to in practice is that plagiarists frequently use words which are much less common than the source author's words to describe something or to talk about something. I refer to the source author as using a 'first line' lexicon: a lexicon of words which are right at the top of consciousness – common, everyday language that most readers can understand. The plagiarist, on the other hand, has only left-overs: 'second line' language, which may not be quite fit for the purpose.

Thus the potential source (Perdue's book) uses – for example – *luxury, sofa and chairs, tumbler* and *chilled*. Brown's book mirrors these strings in *lavish, cushioned chairs, crystal glass* and *fizzing*. Each of these words or phrases is less common than those in Perdue's book. The word *lavish*, for example, occurs with about 1/15[1] of the frequency of *luxury*, while *fizzing* is in roughly the same proportion to *chilled*. This, therefore, raises the question, why would Brown use words which are not from a more common lexicon? We could argue that he is attempting to portray something of a particularly luxurious type: we would naturally imagine that items such as the *oriental carpets*, would support such a contention. Brown appears to have been at pains to paint a particularly evocative scene of wealth and splendour with, for example, the touch about the pewter coffee pot being added to the rest of the list. However, there is at least one argument against this: we are told that the room contains cushioned chairs, oriental carpets and dark oak furniture, in addition to a 'broad desk'. One has the impression of quite a lot of furniture in the room and, having been told that it had the appearance of a 'lavish sitting room at a fine hotel' one would not imagine the room to be cluttered in any sense since this would certainly negate the notion of 'lavish'. One is therefore surprised, on re-reading the excerpt, to see that the room is in fact *small*: this despite the 'broad desk', the 'oriental carpets' (plural) and the 'cushioned chairs' (unspecified number) and the 'dark oak furniture'.

There are two other respects in which I suggest the Brown excerpt shows signs of similarity to the Perdue scene. In the Perdue scene we note the implication that the characters are surprised at what they see: they look silently about them and then inventory the contents of the room for the reader. We cannot be certain that the characters are surprised, but this is certainly one implication of *silently* in this context. In the Brown scene we also gain the impression of surprise because the 'metal and rivets' were 'gone'. It seems as though this was unexpected. Yet surely, it could be argued, a client's viewing room in a traditional Swiss bank, is not likely to contain 'metal and rivets'. As with Perdue's scene, we note that this surprise – if it is surprise – is followed by an inventory of the contents of the room. One wonders why both Perdue and Brown create a scene which conveys luxury in an environment where one would expect luxury, yet both authors appear to cause their characters to be surprised. Or, rather, what one wonders is why Brown's scene is so similar to Perdue's – as seen from the point of view of the characters, why the scene appears to cause each set of characters to behave in very similar ways – that is, not talking but expressing or implying some surprise at a luxury the reader *would* expect. We note also that each excerpt finds closure in the idea of refreshment for the characters in almost identical terms, except that in Perdue's case we have a common 'tumbler', replaced in Brown with the much less common 'crystal glasses'.

The court saga around these questions was nothing if not dramatic. In the New York District Court, Judge Daniels decided to read the books for himself and make up his own mind, despite the evidence I and several other experts, including a literature professor, had submitted. After several months, the judge decided that no plagiarism or copyright infringement had taken place. All of the similarities, in his view, were 'generic' and co-incidental. He therefore ruled that there was no case to answer and dismissed Perdue's claims. Perdue appealed on a number of grounds: first, he said that the judge had misinterpreted some of our evidence, including our claim that the events portrayed by Perdue relating to the Emperor Constantine were not historical record, but fiction. The fact that Brown's interpretation of Constantine was very similar to Perdue's was not simply a matter of repetition of the historical record, but actually repetition of a fiction. The judge had claimed that he was reading the books as an 'ordinary lay reader': we challenged this point, stating that the judge could hardly be equated with 'ordinary lay readers', as his job was to read texts of all kinds on a professional basis. If the judge had really wanted the opinion of ordinary lay readers, why had he not used a jury, or a special reader panel? On this basis the appeal went all the way to the US Supreme Court who, however, upheld the district court's ruling. They decided that the judge had simply followed the law.

The Supreme Court, did, however, return the case to the judge to rule on costs. The judge ruled that Perdue had been right to make his claim, but that the claim was essentially wrong. This meant that Perdue was not responsible for the publisher's costs. Perdue felt vindicated: he stated 'Despite suing me first, Random House and Sony unsuccessfully demanded that I pay the $310,000 in legal fees they spent to sue me.'

Well, it is decision time: time for you, the reader to decide whether, in your view, Brown infringed Perdue's copyright. What do you think?

Note

1. Linguists use large bodies of language to assess word frequencies. Such a body of language is called a 'corpus' (the plural is 'corpora'). We also use internet search engines.

5

THE DIARY THAT TOLD ALL

Between 2002 and 2004 a spate of tyre slashing, paint vandalism and shed arson hit the city of Lincoln. The area around Dixon Street, Knight Street and Shakespeare Street were particularly badly hit. The attacks always took place at night. Residents would wake up to find that several cars in adjacent houses could not be driven owing to the state of their tyres. Others would look out to their garden over breakfast only to see a smouldering wreck where their sheds had once stood. Several car and van owners had their vehicles doused in house paint. The nature of the attacks led detectives and fire experts to conclude that in all likelihood just one person was responsible for the entire crime wave. After months of inquiries that led nowhere and mounting complaints from residents, police eventually received a tip and arrested a local man.

However, despite several hours of questioning, officers were unable to get anywhere with 38-year-old Simon Frederick Barley. He kept telling them that he was suffering from Asperger's Syndrome and that he was not well enough to be questioned. Halfway through one interview he requested to see a doctor. The doctor advised officers not to continue with the questioning. Barley was released on bail and sent home. Some time later a series of diaries stretching back several years was found at his house. Police thought they had struck gold when they realized the diary included descriptions of many of the crimes they were investigating, but Mr Barley was not so easily caught. He denied the crimes and stated that he had compiled the diary only after his arrest, on the premise that since he was being accused he might as well look guilty.

Since the diaries contained a lot of detail about the offences police did not find this explanation entirely plausible and asked Barley where he had got his information from. He said he had looked at old newspapers and spoken to some of the neighbours of those whose vehicles and property had been damaged, and they had given him all the material he needed. Police also pointed out to Barley that the diaries were full of 'normal' entries – visits to the dentist, purchase of a bicycle, shopping trips, family outings, even down to details about what had been bought, who he had met on a particular occasion, where he had been at a certain time and so on. Barley explained that he had copied these entries from his 'proper' diaries for the period and had since destroyed the originals.

For forensic linguists the question of whether one text is contemporaneous with another is particularly interesting. I started my career as a forensic linguist analysing police statements. This is partly due to the police statement protocol that applied pre-1985. Before that time police officers usually began by making notes on suspect admissions and then writing them up into statement form. In the old days, the lack of any external proof that a suspect had actually confessed to a crime caused a number of convicted prisoners to appeal their sentences on the basis that they had been 'verballed', that is, that their words had been altered. However, since the advent of the Police and Criminal Evidence Act (PACE), which allowed for the tape-recording of interviews, the contemporaneity issue was seldom relevant, but there were still a number of old cases around where people had been convicted on the basis of a statement, which some claimed had been fabricated. For example, in one case it was found that the interview notes had been written after the statement was compiled.[1]

In the present case I wondered whether the incriminating entries could be separated from the non-incriminating ones. Diaries are notoriously tricky documents to analyse, simply because they

- can combine formal with informal text;
- can have different addressees (the writer, the diary, an absent friend etc);
- are often written to flatter the writer's self-perception, rather than to be an actual record of events; and
- frequently utilize a combination of narrative, descriptive and monologic strategies.

Based on the above considerations I analysed a number of style features in the diaries:

1. the omission of subject pronouns, for example, 'Met George' in place of 'I met George'; this is of interest because it appears to occur somewhat regularly in the 2003 diary;
2. the use of symbols known as emoticons, such as a smiling face or a frowning face, for example, ☺ and ☹. These appear to have been used to add emphasis to a viewpoint or reaction to a situation;
3. the addition of a drawing to an entry: this can be in the form of a map, a diagram, or a heart, presumably to indicate affection;

4. underlining, apparently to add emphasis to a word or phrase;
5. the use of parentheses, apparently to expand a point, or to de-emphasize non-essential material; and
6. the use of quotation marks to highlight a word or phrase.

For the purposes of general discussion authorship style may be described as a collection of identifying features which occur more or less regularly in a given writer's text. An author acquires a particular style as a result of early language influences, education, social contacts, and exposure to language in various media, such as newspapers, television, films, books and – in many cases – as a result of use of the internet. An author's style can change in some respects over time, probably mostly in terms of the words added to that individual's lexicon (a kind of mental 'word list'). These changes, in an adult's life, can often be attributed to media influences. Variation also occurs as a result of illness, changes in marital status, moving location or switching careers, bereavement, trauma, imprisonment or any other major alteration in an individual's life. Crucially, authorship style is also dependent on topic, register, relationship to the addressee and other contextual factors. Thus, for example, a formal letter by a writer to an employer will exhibit different characteristics from an informal note to a friend.

It thus seemed that if Mr Barley added the material relating to acts of criminality at a later date rather than having written them contemporaneously with the other, non-incriminating, events recorded in his diary, then given (a) that they would have been written at a different time and (b) that they were different in topic from the other entries, it follows that there was a possibility that the types of diary entry – both incriminating and non-incriminating – could be observed through measurement of style features. In other words, we would most likely find that incriminating entries would have style features not shared by non-incriminating ones. After all, we were dealing with a time period of nearly 3 years, a completely different topic range, and possible issues of register and genre.

I then carried out a simple calculation of the frequency of these features across samples of both incriminating and non-incriminating texts. It seemed to me that if distribution across the two sample populations was similar it could add to the possibility that the incriminating entries had been written as an integral part of the diary, and not added – as claimed by Mr Barley – at a later date. On the other hand, if distribution of the features was different between the samples then it would tend to the opposite conclusion. Once I had counted the features I drew up a graph (see Figure 5.1) to be able to visualize the comparison.

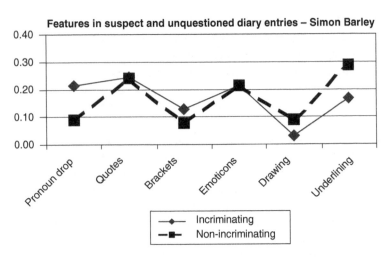

Figure 5.1. Features across the questioned (suspect) and unquestioned samples

As can be seen from the above graph the distribution of the features does not differ greatly from the one type to the other. I should stress that this is not a *statistical* graph. It does not claim to offer evidence of a statistically significant difference between the samples. It is merely a visual aid. From what I had seen, however, I could not say that the difference between the samples seemed substantial: they did not seem to be two different types of entry.

I next looked at the issue of cohesion. Cohesion is a term used by linguists to describe the way a text holds together, a sort of textual glue. A simple example would be 'Fred came into the room. He opened the window'. Here the word 'he' clearly relates back to Fred – unless the writer is being deliberately obscure or misleading. We refer to 'he' as an anaphor and say that it has anaphoric reference to 'Fred'. Anapohoric reference is just one type of cohesion. Other cohesion devices include adverbs of time, for example, *then*, *now*, *before*, adverbs of place, such as *there*, *somewhere* and so on as well as logical relations, for example, *thus*, *so*, *as a result*, etc.

Cohesion occurs in two ways: it can occur within one text, or excerpt – this is internal cohesion. On the other hand it can occur across two texts or excerpts: this is external cohesion. The term external cohesion can also be applied to textual links between different types of text – in this case the incriminating diary entries and the non-incriminating diary entries. So, in the entry for 1 May 2003, Barley writes that he gave his neighbour George a lift home. He is told by George that another neighbour of theirs, call her Mrs Smith, had been telling everybody that Mrs Barley, who was receiving unemployment benefits, was working. On 2 May 2003 Barley tells how he cut off Mrs Smith's communal lighting and threw her bin into the river. In the first entry he refers to Mrs Smith as an 'old swine', and that he was 'furious'. In the second entry he refers to Mrs Smith as an 'old cow' and says that he hates her. Note that the entry of 1 May 2003 is not an incriminating one – it contains no information about any criminal acts. The second entry is an incriminating one: it gives information about something Barley had claimed to have done. Because there is cohesion between the incriminating and non-incriminating entries it becomes harder to believe that the incriminating entries were simply added at a later date – there are strong textual links between the two types of entry here.

In other examples we find descriptions of incriminating entries within ordinary, everyday activities. For example, for 2 June 2003, Barley writes:

Mary's 13th driving lesson ☺

"Stalked the night" No tyres tonight, but set fire to a litter bin on Dixon Street and (from a discreet distance) watched the fire brigade put it out. ☺

Decided not to "stalk the night" any more. I've had enough fun. Posted all the documents J_____ will need to apply for her visa.

In this entry Mr Barley details the criminal activities between two items of non-incriminating text, 'Diana's 13th driving lesson' and 'Posted all the documents'. It would seem that, since the incriminating text is located in this way, then his contention that he added incriminating text to existing entries cannot be supported: here he inserts the incriminating text between two innocuous items. This would imply that the 'original' diary entry – if it existed – had been edited rather than just added to. Moreover, it is curious that he begins his descriptions of the night's activities with a negative 'No tyres tonight'. Since his alleged purpose in writing the incriminating entries was to incriminate himself, it does not make sense to begin with a negative – which is, effectively, a denial. Rather, I suggest that he begins with a negative because the statement in the negative is actually true – that he is simply stating a truth here.

Moreover, the phrase 'decided not to stalk the night anymore' also has implications for the contemporaneity issue. First, it shows a possible association in the diary of the phrase 'stalked the night' with criminal acts or, at the very least, an intent to commit criminal acts (although not every criminal act described in the diary is accompanied by the phrase 'stalked the night'). Secondly, his claim that he decided not to 'stalk the night' anymore is, like the claim relating to 'no tyres tonight', a negative: it describes an intention not to do something. Again, if the incriminating diary entries were about incriminating himself, there would be no reason for Mr Barley to deny an intention to commit a crime. Since we often find the phrase 'stalked the night' occurring in otherwise non-incriminating entries, I suggest that there is no reason to believe that entries containing 'stalked the night' were not contemporaneous with the non-incriminating entries.

As a result of my analysis I could not find anything in the diary entries for the year 2003 to suggest Mr Barley did not record the events as they occurred. Thus I concluded that there was nothing to support the contention that the incriminating material was added later. For this reason little credence could be given to the claim that there was an earlier diary which had been destroyed by Mr Barley. It seemed that Mr Barley had written his diary entries as one production: nothing had been added later, as he had claimed.

Eventually, Mr Barley 'came clean' and admitted to 35 incidents of tyre slashing and 19 incidents of arson, in addition to sundry other criminal acts, such as destroying a van by throwing a tin of house paint over it. Lincoln Crown Court had no hesitation in finding him guilty, but to date sentencing has been held up because of his claimed medical condition, which is why I have had to use a pseudonym for him here.

Note

1. In the case of Carl Bridgewater, murdered in 1978. One of the suspects, Pat Molloy, claimed he did not dictate his statement but parts of it were 'fed' to him and he was also asked questions. Later, ESDA analysis confirmed that the notes had followed, rather than preceded, the statement. See *Times Law Report*, 22 February 1997.

6

THE MAN WITH THE BASEBALL BAT

Imagine you are about 17 years old and someone threatens you with a baseball bat. If this were not bad enough, imagine also that you are blind. One morning your mobile phone rings. You answer it and this is what you hear: 'I have a baseball bat for your kneecaps,' the voice at the other end says.

The background to the case was that two youths at a blind school in the south of England got into an argument with each other about a girl. Angry words were exchanged between the boys and there was a lot of bad feeling between them. The school did its best to sort the problem out but nothing was resolved and eventually one of the boys left the school. The boy who remained at the school was the one who received the threatening call. He believed that the voice belonged to the father of the other boy. The police were called and interviewed the suspect.

The boy who made the complaint had had the presence of mind to record the conversation as it took place. He had previously received an anonymous call and was almost ready for it. Being able to do this when you are blind takes not only ingenuity but a cool head as well, especially if you are being threatened at the same time.

The telephone call had also been made on a mobile phone, with the caller's number being suppressed. This is something you can do on a phone in the United Kingdom quite easily. However, in some countries it is not possible. The fact that the recording was from a mobile phone onto a mobile phone meant that the sound quality of the call was poorer than it would probably have been had the call been placed from a landline. My instructions from the police force[1] where the offence took place were straightforward: was the anonymous caller the same person as the known speaker?

For the reader who is interested in how this kind of inquiry is handled, you can break a voice identification down into a number of separate headings:

- First, are the two samples apparently of the same dialect/accent?
- Secondly, are the voices of the same type?

- Thirdly, if we look at pronunciation of certain speech sounds (called 'phonemes') are they similar across the known and questioned voices?

As regards the first point, the voices both shared the same dialect, actually from the North West of Wales. One feature of this dialect is the way many speakers pronounce the sound 'k'. It is not unlike the way some Scottish speakers pronounce the last sound in the word 'loch'. It is partly produced towards the back of the mouth in an area known as the velum, hence the term 'velar sound'. This sound appeared in the word 'kneecaps', 'college', and also in the word 'got'. The 'g' sound in 'got' is similar to 'k', except that when you say 'g' you actually vibrate your vocal cords, but when you say 'k' you do not. Try it and see. As you can hear, aside from the presence or absence of the vocal cords, it is the same sound. In the interview the suspect, referring to his son, said 'he doesn't know whether he's coming or going'. The velar sound appeared in both these words in the 'k' and the 'g'. However, although we find the velar 'k' and 'g' in this speaker's dialect, in the case of this speaker it was particularly strong. In my view it was much stronger than is usually the case. I felt this was distinctive.

Another interesting feature of this speaker was the way he pronounced words like 'speak'. At one point in the phone call he taunts the blind boy by saying 'Speak to me'. When he says 'speak' he actually says 'sbeak'. On listening to the word 'kneecaps' I noticed the same phenomenon, 'kneecabs'. In the course of his police interview the suspect said, again referring to the time period of which his son and the other boy had been at loggerheads with each other, 'over a period of years'. Here, the word 'period' sounded more like 'beriod'.

The next question to consider was whether the voices were of the same type. Phoneticians use a number of descriptors for voice types. At one end of the spectrum you have a voice like Marilyn Monroe – especially when at its most persuasive. Listening to a voice like this you have the overwhelming impression of being 'soft-soaped' or seduced by the speaker. What you are listening to, for the most part, is simply breath. The vocal cords are wide open and the breath is continuous. It's like a constant rush of air. Hence phoneticians talk about a 'breathy' voice. At the opposite end of the spectrum you have a voice which sounds not unlike a door creaking. You may remember Dr Kissinger, the globetrotting Secretary of State for the United States of America back in the 1970s. His voice would literally creak as he talked. Try it yourself. How you do it, is to lower your voice as much as possible and say 'aah'. Listen to the creak in the voice. Not surprisingly, such a voice is known as a 'creaky' voice. Here the vocal cords are almost completely closed off at one end. The actor Humphrey Bogart tended to have a creaky voice, and you will often hear media pundits with such a voice. It is also known as the 'expert's' voice. Do not imagine, however, that only men have a voice like this: women can also have creaky voices. In the same way, you will also find men with breathy voices. A good example was the actor Derek Nimmo. In case these names are unfamiliar to you, if you are near a computer, do a search on Youtube. You will find many references to each of the people I have named here and you will be able to listen to the voices for yourself.

Right in the middle of *breathy* and *creaky* you have the normal, modal voice. This is what our suspect had: a completely middle of the road way of producing his voice – with, however, one exception. The voice was very tense, perhaps even stressed. This did not appear to be just because he was in a stressful situation, either on the phone or in the police interview room. It seemed to be a quality that was always there.

In the police interview he repeatedly denied having made the threatening phone call. However, based on the number of similarities across the known and questioned voices, I felt there was a high probability that it was him, and said so in my report. He continued to deny responsibility for a while, but then – as sometimes happens – changed his mind when he got to court, and decided to plead. The court found him guilty of sending a malicious communication, which is a serious offence and he was fined heavily. The magistrate said that had it not been for his age and health, the consequences for him might have been more serious.

At about the same time I began another voice identification from North Wales. A couple had been burgled at about 2 a.m. near Wrexham. Raiders had stolen credit cards, mobile phones and the couple's car. High on a cocktail of drinks and drugs the perpetrators had driven the car recklessly through the town, throwing out personal possessions they had found in the vehicle, including the male victim's works uniform. They then trashed the couple's car and left it on a housing estate. A little later the burglars received a phone call. The voice at the other end appeared to be the female victim, but what the burglars did not know was that they were actually speaking to a police officer. She very cleverly constructed the conversation to get the maximum amount of conversation out of the two young men. This is very helpful in voice identification cases, where you need as wide a range of speech sounds, indications of vocal expression and voice dynamic as possible.

Based on knowledge of the local criminal fraternity police officers thought they recognized the voices and the following morning several homes were raided in the Wrexham vicinity, including that of Andrew Caveney, aged 23 and Daniel Roberts, aged 21. Along with the conversation with the burglars in the car, I also received the interview tapes, one with each of the suspects.

The sound quality on interview tapes differs greatly from that found in phone calls, especially mobile phone calls. Interviews are conducted in what are known as PACE rooms. PACE stands for the Police And Criminal Evidence Act. It was introduced in 1985 to regulate, amongst other things, the way suspects and witnesses are interviewed by police in criminal cases. Prior to this, PACE interviews were not taped, but were written down in note form and then compiled into statements. This caused many suspects to claim that they had been 'verballed' by officers. Verballing is the process whereby a statement is altered to 'fit' someone up. The tape-recording of interviews has put a stop to most verballing claims since, if the quality of the sound on the tape is clear enough, usually there is no dispute as to what was said.

In contrast to the quality found on most interview tapes, mobile phones usually present the voice analyst with problems of clarity, signal interference and environmental noise. In the present instance the suspects were talking while driving. A moving vehicle is not the best place to try to identify a voice, especially if the car is being driven with the windows open.

Both of the voices appeared to be from the Wrexham area. The elder male's voice was particularly distinctive when pronouncing words like 'back' and 'smack'. At one point he tells the caller that she is lucky he did not come upstairs to her bedroom and wake her up. He says he often does this and enjoys giving his female victims a good 'smack' or 'slap'. I found this speaker's voice very distinctive: he had a loud, harsh voice with a nasal quality, which was evident both in the tape and the police interview.

The second voice was also very distinctive. The speaker appeared to have a stammer and often garbled his sentences in particular ways. Only about 3 per cent of the population have any kind of stammer, and it is not always accompanied by grammatical problems, which was the case here. Evidently, this was a very nervous speaker who, once he began to stammer, would then mangle up his grammar by putting in words which did not belong, and even inventing words on occasion.

Had the crime not been so serious the PACE interviews with the two perpetrators would have been amusing. Their efforts to deny their crime bordered on the inventively pathological. They fabricated the most marvellous excuses as to their whereabouts. However, their voices betrayed them completely. They finally admitted to their crimes when presented with the voice evidence and were sentenced to 3 years' imprisonment.

Note

1. To protect the victim in this instance I am not revealing any identifiable details of this case.

7

REPUTABLE BARRISTER OR MANIPULATIVE SVENGALI?

This case involved a claim by tenants of a property belonging to a barrister. The claim was that the barrister had used undue influence in attempting to persuade them to rent the property from him. In support of their claim the tenants produced several witnesses who were supposed to have remembered, independently of each other, the 'exact' words of the barrister, several years after he had allegedly said them.

The barrister, who lived in the east of England, had rented out the property to a care home company owned by Mr and Mrs Artemis. After a while, the care home company stopped paying rent to the barrister, Mr Wheeler. On ceasing to receive rental for his property, Mr Wheeler sued his tenants. The tenants counterclaimed that Mr Wheeler had made false representations to them, in effect inducing them to enter into the leasing of his property. Mr Wheeler, a retired barrister with an impeccable record was stunned at this allegation. Among their witnesses the tenants produced a local shopkeeper and his assistant. These witnesses claimed that Mr Wheeler had asked them to persuade the tenants to enter into the lease with him and to purchase the care home from its previous owners. Mr Wheeler submitted copies of the witness and defendant statements which contained examples of the language used by the defendants and their witnesses. Among the claims by the defence were these alleged quotations of Mr Wheeler's in his efforts to ensure that his property was leased by Mr and Mrs Artemis:

- a. '. . . it's a very *good* thriving nursing home and an opportunity not to be missed . . .'
- b. 'You will be missing out on a *good* opportunity . . .'
- c. That the care home 'was a *good* little business . . .'
- d. '. . . was a *good* business opportunity not to be missed . . .'
- e. '. . . that the property was in a *good* state of repair . . .'

What interested me from the outset about these quotations was that they were supposed to be quotations at all. How was it that the tenants used direct quotations and so did their witnesses? How was it that the wording was so alike? It seemed to be clearly the case that the defence were intending to signify that (a) to (e) were direct representations of Mr Wheeler's words, that is to say the exact words he supposedly used. This raised several important issues, including, the nature of 'lawyer' language, the limitations of memory for exact wordings, the generic quality of the quoted wordings and the supposedly persuasive content of the words themselves.

In general, I have found lawyers to be somewhat cautious in their use of language, especially lawyers of Mr Wheeler's generation. Not only are they usually cautious about the content, but they are also somewhat conservative about the kinds of structures they use. Thus, in the present instance I would find it somewhat surprising for a barrister to say something like 'a very good thriving nursing home and an opportunity not to be missed', since (a) the first clause renders the second virtually redundant and (b) the qualifications to the noun phrase 'nursing home' are somewhat awkward in structure, namely, 'very good thriving'. In addition, I also find the phrase 'very good thriving nursing home' something of a tongue-twister and not easy to say aloud, especially when 'and an opportunity not to be missed' is added to it. In fact, it has more of a written than a spoken feel about it. Moreover, most lawyers have a wide vocabulary, by reason of education, training and experience. I would be surprised if a senior lawyer of more than 30 years' experience at the bar, who was also a graduate in English from Oxford and had a higher degree in Economics, was not able to offer anything more apt than 'good'. Some of the expressions even border on the trite, for example, 'good little business'. All in all it did not seem credible that a lawyer would use this kind of language – not once, but on a number of occasions. It certainly bore little resemblance to the telephone conversations I had had with Mr Wheeler, and even less with his written correspondence, which was invariably measured and sober, one would even say a little dull.

It is not controversial among linguists that memory for exact wording of what has been said is poor. Contrary to popular belief, most people are unable to remember their exact words even a few minutes after having said them. Many psychologists and linguists have reported on this phenomenon, including MacWhinney et al. (1982),[1] Hjelmquist (1984)[2] and others. In an experiment undertaken for an appeal court hearing in Scotland in the famous Ice Cream Wars, a psychologist challenged the claim that four police officers were able to remember having heard a suspect saying 'I only wanted the van windows shot up. The fire at Fat Boy's was only meant to be a frightener which went too far.' The officers allegedly noted this phrase down independently of each other some time after it was supposed to have been said. Professor Brian Clifford, a cognitive psychologist specializing in memory undertook an experiment to test people's memory for language. In his evidence to the appeal court, Clifford said that most cognitive psychologists were agreed that the upper limit on short term memory, whether for language or – for example – numbers, was approximately seven but unlikely to be more than nine discrete items. Beyond that, in the case of language, meaning would be retained, but not the actual words themselves (paraphrased from the Appeal Court hearing[3]).

Professor Clifford carried out an experiment involving 57 participants of mixed social profile (age, class, occupation). One group was given contextual information about the claimed utterance, the other was not. The participants were asked to write down something which would be said to them, being the claimed statement of the police officers given above, that is, 'I only wanted the van windows shot up. The fire at Fat Boy's was only meant to be a frightener which went too far.' The experiment showed, first, that not one of the participants was able to recall verbatim what was said to them. There was not much difference between the recall of the group which had contextual information and those which did not. The average recall level was between 30 and 40 per cent. This is in line with experiments undertaken by other psychologists and linguists. Even a few seconds after being asked to remember someone's words, the exact wording is unlikely to be reproduced, especially if it is longer than seven or eight words. Contrast this with the claims of the defendants and their witnesses in this case: the longest phrase is 14 words in length, and it is claimed to have been remembered verbatim several years afterwards, that is, 'It's a very good thriving nursing home and an opportunity not to be missed.' This is particularly surprising when we consider the defendants' memory for times and dates which appear somewhat poor, even when relating to important matters such as the dates of negotiations, with phrases like 'on several occasions', 'a later discussion', 'later proved to be untrue' and so on. I asked Mr Wheeler to try to obtain accounts in the defendants' own words – unaided – either written or spoken, but preferably spoken. However, the defendants and their witnesses, on the advice of their solicitor, declined to provide this information.

The claimed exact memory for the wordings listed above is all the more remarkable when one considers that the wordings themselves are entirely unexceptional. They are in fact somewhat generic with 'opportunity', 'business' and 'good' appearing several times. In support of the generic nature of these phrases, most corpus studies will reveal that 'good' and 'opportunity' are high frequency collocates, as are 'missed' and 'opportunity'. Typical examples of generic language used in cases where veracity is at issue include precise times (e.g. 9 a.m., 5.30 etc), exact periods of time (e.g. 18 months, a fortnight etc), generic personal aliases (e.g. John Smith, Fred Brown etc), generic meals (e.g. 'pizza and chips') and generic excuses (e.g. 'my car wouldn't start', 'I had a headache' etc). The defendants claimed that Mr Wheeler's words swayed them into buying the business and renting his property. Persuasive language uses any of a number of linguistic resources to induce, allure or influence, including rhetorical and poetic devices such as alliteration, rhyme, connotation, the use of keywords and so on. Yet the quotations given above contain no such elements, or any other specific methods of persuasion that I could think of. The only adjectives are 'good' and 'thriving', other than 'little'. This word interested me in the context of persuasion: a 'good little business' is one in which the proprietor makes what we might consider a 'reasonable' living. It is hardly a term one would apply to a business with a turnover of over two million pounds a year. In this context I would have expected phrases such as 'substantial', 'well-established', with references to reputation, efficiency, standing in the community and so on. On its own 'thriving' can be a powerful word, but accompanied by 'very good' I suggest the effect is somewhat vitiated.

Even if Mr Wheeler may have said some of the above to either the prospective purchasers or others of his acquaintance, who was to say that he was making any attempt to be more persuasive than any other businessman would be under the circumstances? As common sense questions we can surely ask ourselves if it is unusual for a seller to attempt to persuade someone to buy something, and whether – even if it was unusual – would this be sufficient reason to withhold the entire rental value on a property for several years? In their verdict on the issue the court ruled that there were no grounds for believing that Mr Wheeler had acted unethically or unscrupulously, and certainly not illegally. The judge's view was that the claims by the defendants were no more than a cynical ploy to avoid the just payment of their obligations and found in favour of Mr Wheeler. The tenants were ordered to pay damages and to clear the arrears on their rent.

Notes

1. MacWhinney B., Keenan J. M. and P. Reinke (1982). 'The role of arousal in memory for conversation'. *Memory & Cognition* Vol. 10 (4), 308–317.
2. Hjelmquist E. (1984). 'Memory for conversations'. *Discourse Processes*, 7, 321–336.
3. XC956/03, XC959/03, XC958/03, High Court of Justiciary, Glasgow, before Lords Justice Clerk, MacLean and Macfadyen, 17 March 2004.

Part 2

8

MURDER OR SUICIDE?

About 4 years ago Walter, a young man in one of the southern states of the United States of America, died from gunshot wounds. According to the girl he was with on the Friday evening in question, he had pulled a gun out of his pocket, inserted the barrel into his mouth and shot himself in front of her. He was 19 years of age. One evening, several weeks before the shooting, the boy had come home and told his mother he did not want to see Tracy anymore. Asked why he wanted to end a relationship that had lasted nearly 3 years, Walter replied that her family was mixed up in 'something bad' and wanted him to be involved as well. He had refused. After this Tracy kept phoning and texting Walter to reconsider being with her. Because Walter's mother thought the girl and her parents had been pressuring her son so much just before his death, she found it difficult to believe that Walter had killed himself. To her mind, it was much more likely that Walter had been killed by the girl's family. The mother's suspicions were raised when the local county sheriff refused to open an investigation, stating that in his view – backed up by the county coroner's post-mortem – that the death was clearly suicide. What was more, a letter had been found in the boy's jeans pocket, and in the sheriff's view it was a suicide note.

> Please give anything I own to Mike and Pete. Tell both of them I love them so much. Mike, you're goanna really be something buddy. You're good at sports, handsome, and really smart. You keep up the good work man and you can do anything you want. I'm sorry for always picking on you, but I was always just joking, I love you with all of my heart and I'm sorry if I ever hurt your feelings man. You mean the world to me. I'm so sorry. And to Pete you are goanna be great to man. You are the toughest little kid I know. You are to cute and smart. Keep hitting homeruns and do good in school. You better listen to Momma and Dad. I know you're probably to young to understand man, but always remember that Walter loves you more than anything. I'm so sorry. I really wish I would've spent

more time with yall, but I did not and am so sorry. Momma I appreciate everything you did for me. I can never thank you enough. You never turned on me for no reason, you always helped me. I love you so much. Please forgive me I'm so sorry. I could've never asked for a better mom. I know I probably never told you enough but I really love you

After the county sheriff refused to investigate further, I was contacted by the deceased's relatives and asked whether there was any way of telling whether the note was a suicide note. I asked them if there were any other examples of Walter's use of language – either from a computer or in his own handwriting. After making inquiries, they said it was rare for the boy to write anything. Thus, I had only a single text to examine and nothing to compare it with. One way to find out whether a letter is a suicide note is to try to discover what genuine suicide notes have in common with each other, and how they might differ from fake suicide notes. Normally, linguists do not ask questions relating to motive. It is really a question for psychologists. However, in the case of suicide notes it may be worth making an exception. The reason for doing so, however, is not to probe personal motive as such, but, eventually, to arrive at a linguistic understanding of suicide notes.

Back in 1957 the famous suicidologist – in fact the founder of the science – Edwin Shneidman, researched the background to hundreds of suicides, including the types of relationship victims had had with their families. He noticed that the first question almost all of the victim's friends and family asked after being informed of a suicide was 'Why?'. This question, perhaps obvious at first, is very revealing. In addition to the obvious implication that relatives cannot understand why their loved ones have killed themselves, there is another implication: that the deceased's behaviour was irrational. Hence, what relatives say and think after a suicide is important. While the initial reaction may be puzzlement, this can soon turn to anger and they may begin to think of the person as crazy, often using such expressions as 'cowardly', a 'loser' and so on. It is useful to know about this not uncommon sequence of grief reactions because, in turn, it tells us something of the way in which the general public view suicide. Once we know what this popular view of suicide is we can to some extent predict what a fake suicide note will tend to look like: it will reflect popular attitudes such as that suicidal people are 'crazy', 'cowardly' and so on. So, what I am suggesting is that in order to understand something about genuine suicide notes we first need to understand something about fake ones. After analysing many suicide notes, it seemed to me that fake notes often contained the same kinds of expression that grieving and bemused relatives used: 'crazy', 'cowardly' and so on. People who write fake suicide notes – for whatever reason – are probably just as much in the dark as relatives trying to understand the motivation for suicide in their loved ones. It occurred to me that a kind of *diglossia* was at work in suicide notes. Diglossia (which means 'two languages') is a term first used by the Greek linguist, Yannis Psycharis[1] (1854–1929). He was speaking about two forms of Greek, the prestige form used by the ruling classes and the common form used by everybody else. The prestige form of Greek was known as Katharevousa, while the language spoken by most people was Demotic Greek (the Greek of the people). For speakers of demotic Greek the prestige language was an outsider's language, almost another language. What I am suggesting in the case of suicide notes is that the fake suicide note is also in the language of the 'outsider', and not in the language of the person intending to commit suicide, the genuine 'insider'.

We would therefore expect that fake suicide notes will mostly contain 'outsider' views of suicide – in other words, the kinds of populist views we have been describing above, in opposition to genuine suicide notes which we would expect to contain language truly reflective of suicide. In principle, this may seem a relatively simple idea, but the question you are probably asking at this stage is how this might work out in practice. This is where the work of Shneidman has proved valuable. Following from his earlier work, mentioned above, he observed that the act of suicide is the direct result of 'the constriction, the concentration, the tunneling of vision, the pathological narrowing and focus on the Self that is a usual part of the suicidal state' (Shneidman 2004: 162).

Thus, what happens in suicide, according to Shneidman, is that victims become so obsessed and focused on a situation that they are unable to think outside of the tunnel – the problem in effect encloses them and they are literally unable to see a way out of it. The language they produce in this situation is thus truly 'insider' language. It is as though the person is in a war situation, holed up in a bunker completely alone, unable to communicate their situation except through the suicide note. A nurse who had previously thought of suicide as weak and cowardly changed her mind after attempting suicide herself:[2] 'I have been a nurse for years and if asked I would have told you that those who commit suicide are weak, cowardly and selfish.' And, still on the subject of 'weakness' Dr Dainius Puras, a psychiatrist from Lithuania found that this reaction was not uncommon: 'There is a lot of cynical thinking in Eastern block countries. That it is maybe better to let the weak die.'[3] Internet searches show that words like 'weak', 'cowardly', 'insane', 'crazy', 'nuts' and 'mad' (in the UK sense of the word) regularly co-occur with reference to suicide. Evidently, the notion that suicides are weak people unable to face their difficulties is widespread.

Back in 1957 Shneidman, and a colleague of his by the name of Norman Farberow had taken the unusual step of asking a carefully selected group of their patients to write fake suicide notes. The patients were instructed to use pseudonyms, such as Bill or Joe. Thirty-three of their patients agreed to take part in the experiment, and Shneidman and Farberow then compared these fake notes with a selection of 33 notes provided by the local county coroner's office, matched for age, gender, type of occupation and so on. What they found was very revealing in terms of linguistically expressed motives for suicide.

It is commonly thought that only genuine suicides apologize to their family and friends for committing suicide. However, in the Shneidman Farberow corpus there is no difference between the numbers of those who apologize and those who do not. Similarly, there is little difference between the numbers who ask for forgiveness and those who do not. Genuine suicides are only a little less likely to ask for forgiveness than their fake counterparts. The majority of expressions of love, and claims to have loved, come from genuine texts, and these kinds of expression are rare in fake texts. Phrases claiming that the victim's survivors are 'wonderful' are in about the same proportion – very few fakes in other words praise their surviving relatives. On the negative side high numbers of genuine suicides state an inability to cope with life, with the phrases 'can't stand' and 'can't take' proving common. Similarly, many claim to have been feeling 'bad' – often about something they did, or they make reference, in the same terms, to their health. There are not infrequent mentions of having hurt someone, either physically or emotionally. A small number ascribe blame to their survivor or survivors. Hence, the picture that emerges is one of emotional ambivalence: the victim often praises the loved one but also blames them, asks for forgiveness, but simultaneously expresses intolerance, makes avowals of love, but also indicates feelings of 'badness'.

On the other hand, references to death, 'the end', being 'deceased' and so on are rare in fake notes and tend to prevail in genuine ones. In the same texts, there are not infrequent expressions of fatigue and even comments about having 'tried' to please a partner or other family members. We also find in genuine texts, directive and prescriptive strategies – things that the loved one who is being written to must and must not do. As noted before, references to weakness, cowardliness and insanity are much more likely to occur in fake notes than genuine ones, and this is also borne out by the Shneidman Farberow corpus.

I also obtained a corpus of suicide notes from the British Transport Police. I did this because even though Shneidman and Farberow had researched the circumstances of the victims of their genuine notes very thoroughly, it was still possible that one or two of these people may not have committed suicide. On the other hand it was equally possible that one or two of those who wrote fake notes for the research, may have gone on to commit suicide later. Hence, what I was looking for was a body of notes which were indisputably genuine. The answer came from British Transport Police because, unfortunately, every year a number of people jump in front of British trains in order to commit suicide. Many of these people leave a note at home, or a note is found on them after their death. Since there are always several witnesses to these deaths, because they usually happen at busy times when a number of people are present on the station platform, it is indisputable that the victim has committed suicide. Therefore, in reading these notes, we cannot doubt that the victim is a genuine suicide. In turn, there is no reason for doubting that the suicide note found on the victim or at their home is also a genuine text. The data from these texts is strikingly similar to the data from the genuine notes Shneidman and Farberow collected from the county coroner's office, showing that they had done their research into the victims' lives and deaths with true academic dedication and thoroughness. We find many of the same expressions in the railway suicides as in the Shneidman Farberow corpus, such as 'can't stand', 'can't take', 'have loved', 'wonderful' and so on. When we compare the railway texts with the genuine texts the overall profile is very similar.

The key finding of all of the genuine texts, including the railway texts, is that the populist conceptions held by the general public about suicide, are not found in the genuine texts.

Turning back to the text written by Walter, which I have quoted in full above, we note many signs of 'insider' language, including praise for his younger brothers, apologies to them for what has happened, expressions of love for his mother and other members of his family, requests to give his property to Pete and Mike and instructions to the two boys to obey their parents. In addition to many of the hallmarks of 'insider' language, we find an apparent absence of the types of 'outsider' language I was referring to: there is no mention of being weak or crazy, of being insane, of seeking an easy way out and there is no mention of mental confusion or cowardliness. After some consideration, therefore it seemed to me that the note sent to me by Walter's mother was more likely to be a suicide note than not. I reported this to the mother's relatives and they thanked me for my time and effort. They felt that as a result she would be able to find some closure to this episode in her life.

Notes

1. Psycharis, G. (1988). *To Taxidi mou*. Athens: Nefeli.
2. Found at: http://www.sowingseedsoffaith.com/suicide.answers.htm on 22 May 2008.
3. Found at: http://www.insightnewstv.com/d74 on 22 May 2008.

9

WHAT HAPPENED TO JENNY?

In June 2005, 19-year-old Jenny Nicholl disappeared from her home town of Richmond in Yorkshire. Known as a home-loving teenager with plenty of local friends and workmates, the disappearance was a complete mystery to her family and friends. Several appeals were made for notification of her whereabouts, including heart-rending appeals by her parents. However, all of this was to no avail, except that Jenny's parents continued to receive mobile phone texts from her phone for some time. Police were concerned that Jenny's disappearance might not have been voluntary and wondered if the texts sent from Jenny's phone might be from someone who may have abducted her. Was there a particular date, for example, when a style change within the texts became evident?

One way to find style changes is to begin by considering individual words and phrases which can be written in more than one way, for example 'I am' vs. 'I'm', 'two' vs. '2' and so on. In the mobile phone text environment there are many such choices, such as 'av', 'hav' and 'ave' for 'have', the dropping of the final 'g' in words ending in '-ing', 'of' for 'off', 'fone' for 'phone' and so on. We can simplify this task of finding alternative lexical choices by classifying them under different headings, such as in Table 9.1.

I found a number of instances where more than one possible selection in a given context had been used across the texts, for example word final '-ing' was found to be written as both '-ing' and '-in' and I found instances of 'have' occurring both as 'have' and 'ave'. The 15 texts from Jenny's phone were placed in chronological order, to see if there was a point in the sequence at which a significant number of dualities (or choices) would be evident. This would in theory imply that there was a cut off point, either side of which a distinctive style might become apparent. This in turn would lend credence to the view that the texts were two styles, and therefore that the texts might possibly be by two authors. However, in doing this I needed to bear in mind a number of points, including the following:

- A person's style of writing or texting can change if, for example, s/he undergoes changes in life circumstances (such as moving away from

Table 9.1. Classification of alternative lexical choices

Type of potential choice	Description	Example
Morphological	Alteration of inflections attached to words	-ed, -ing, un-, etc
Alphanumeric	Use of numbers for words or parts of words	'4' for 'four', etc
Letter replacive	Use of letters for words or parts of words	'c' for 'see'
Orthographic (homophonic)	Use of similar sounding phonemes, syllables or words	'fone' for 'phone'
Orthographic (punctuation)	Avoidance of punctuation, lack of space between words or after punctuation, issues of case	R u goin2?See ya
Orthographic (case)	Not using upper case for first letter of sentence or first letter of proper nouns	is bev dere
Orthographic/Phonic reduction	Using a simplified spelling	'fink' for 'think', 'dere' for 'there'

family and friends, changing jobs, etc), begins a course of medication, is emotionally upset, forms new relationships and so on. Text type and addressee relationship also play an important part in influencing text styles.

• Determining different styles of language on the basis of small samples is itself fraught with difficulties. A language feature which occurs in a small sample cannot be depended on to be a 'constant' (in fact true constants even in large language samples are difficult to glean useful measurements from). It is highly possible that if the language sample were larger, several variations of that feature would be exhibited.

I then made a comprehensive list of all the possible textual dualities I could observe, which were as shown in Table 9.2. The rationale for feature selection was based on observation of the texts rather than on any a-priori criteria for reasons of sample size and textual type. Thus, if we were comparing two novels we would be able to list many features which presented the opportunity for dualities, but in the case of a small mobile phone corpus the opportunities for dualities will clearly be limited. However, cell phone texts sometimes use mixed styles, and so we cannot always be sure if we are seeing normal variation or duality of authorship. If you examine Table 9.2, you will see that of the 13 features tested 8 exhibited differences between the earlier and later texts, but some of these appear in both earlier and later texts.

Table 9.2. List of feature dualities tested

Word	Written as	Text Number
have	have	2
have	ave	12,15
ing	ing	4,5,5,8,11,12,12,12,13,13,13,15,15,15
ing	in	1,1,4,14,14,14
off	off	6,9,14
off	of	13
phone	phone	13
phone	fone	6,8
shit	shit	1,4,12,15
shit	shite	13,14
you	u	1,3,5,7,7,8,8,8,9,10,12,14,14
you	y	14
you	ya	12
good	good	8
good	gud	2
doesn't	doesnt	8
doesn't	dont	13
I am	i am	13,13,13,14,15,15
I am	im	6,7,9,11
I u.c.*		12
my	my	2,8,11,13
my	me	12,13,13,15,15

*(u.c. = upper case)

In addition to the above categories, two other orthographic features were tested, the omission of a vowel between two consonants, for example, 'lve' for 'leave' and the incorporation of a digit into a phrase or clause, for example, 'had2go' as opposed to 'had 2 go'.

I found that the omitted vowel in words like 'leave' was not significant, but that on the other hand the situation where an alpha number (e.g. '2' for 'two') was not attached to the word on either side was significant. The earlier texts mostly showed phenomena like 'want2go' rather than 'want 2 go'. There were several of these groupings of two or more words into clusters, that is, expressions without spaces between the words, including 'suppose2go'. This is by no means idiosyncratic since many people use this kind of feature in their cell phone texts, but at the same time the later texts showed fewer instances of it. The average length of these cluster words fell markedly from those texts dated after Jenny's disappearance, from 6.16 characters to 4.09 characters (letters and numbers). Texts up to the date in question (26 June 2005) contain long clusters such as 'suppose2go', 'cu2moz', 'icant2day' and so on, but after that date the clusters are in general shorter, for example, 'iam' 'every1', 'm8' and so on. It is not just the case that the earlier texts demonstrate a longer (on average) cluster, but the cluster is different in character. The earlier clusters tend to be phrases or clauses, whereas the later clusters are usually single words, or perhaps two words at the most. Thus, in the earlier clusters we get, for example, 'booked2go', 'want2go', 'have2get', whereas in the later clusters the infinitive verb is usually separate from the main verb and particle, for example, 'ave2 go' (twice). Moreover, we find no phrases such as 'present-2moz' (present tomorrow), 'and2will's', or clauses such as 'cu2moz' or 'go2shop'. There therefore seem to be two distinct ways of clustering words. The earlier clusters usually have an alphanumeric centrally placed, usually '2'. The later clusters often have no attachment to the alphanumeric on the right side. I considered this feature to be significant.

I next looked at the length of each of the texts. Word count was measured in two ways: firstly words as actual words, for example, in 'cu2moz' the actual word count would be three words, 'c u 2moz'. Words counted in cluster formation, that is, where 'cu2moz' is counted as one word, were also computed. In both types of word count, texts before 26 June 2005 were on average much shorter than after that date. It therefore appeared that the earlier texts were significantly shorter than the later texts. This feature, too, seemed to be significant.

I then considered word length average. To an extent this has been dealt with under the topic of clusters above but, additionally, word length average is noticeably different for cluster word count (5.44 before/4.77 after), but is not noticeably different for actual word count (3.59 before/3.57 after). The latter measure is a low word length average, which probably reflects the informal nature of the content of many cell phone texts. Mobile phone texts often exhibit low word length averages.

I wondered whether the issue of linguistic register would be important in the present case. In simple terms, register is the degree of formality in a text. In very broad terms, we could say 'I am' is more formal than 'I'm'. For the purposes of this discussion, 'I am', for example, would be said to be in a higher register than 'I'm'. There is no noticeable register change between the earlier texts and the later texts. This is because the register in both is mixed: we have formal register words with less formal register words in both text sets. For example, the earlier texts tend to write 'my' as 'my' (including 'myself') which is formal, while 'I am' is written in the earlier texts mostly as 'im' and in the later texts as 'i am' which is more formal, while 'my' in the later texts is written mostly as 'me' (including 'meself'). The fact that one construction is formal in the early texts and informal later, with the opposite being true of the other construction is probably not significant. As indicated above, it is not unusual to find mixed registers in one individual's cell phone texts, even in a single text. However, as both constructions self-reference the writer/texter, it is interesting that there is a change in self-referencing style in the later texts. Regrettably, the importance of this point cannot be assessed in linguistic terms except that we could say that 'my' is usually more stressed phonetically than 'me' (when 'my' is meant), and that 'I am' stresses the verb 'am', whereas in 'I'm' it is the pronoun which is apparently being stressed. The main point here was that there was no register difference between the earlier and later texts, but that this is not surprising, given that cell phone texts generally tend to exhibit a mixture of registers. Hence, register did not seem to be significant. However, it did seem to me that there was a change in texting style in the texts dated after 26 June 2005. I was informed after sending in my report that Jenny had last been definitively sighted on the 30 June 2005.

As I mentioned above, I was dealing with a very small sample of language here, and felt that there was a need to treat the result with some caution. There could be all sorts of perfectly valid explanations for the differences. For example, alterations in one's life circumstances, relational changes and major emotional disturbances can all cause style changes in one's use of language. In the context of a disappearance, this is not unrealistic: the later texts purport to be from a teenager who has left home, has apparently taken up a new relationship, appears to be angry with her parents and wishes to be left alone and so on. It is possible that all of the differences between the earlier and later texts could be explained in this way, in the context of changes in texter-addressee relationships. The increased length of the texts, however, is puzzling, unless one takes into account the fact that the content of the later texts is totally different from that of the earlier texts, and that two of the later texts are purportedly addressed to a parent rather than to a member of Jenny's peer group, which was the norm for the earlier texts. Also, whereas the earlier texts refer to meetings with friends, or plans to meet, short discussions of a friend's birthday, a reference to present whereabouts and so on, the later texts are in the main apparently designed to explain a lengthy absence from home and might therefore feasibly require to be longer. However, on balance it seemed that there were just too many differences to be explained by coincidence.

It was over 2 years after working on this case that the trial of David Hodgson took place at Teesside Crown Court. He was found guilty of Jenny's murder, but unfortunately her body has never been recovered, and Hodgson continues to disavow any participation in the crime.

10

A CASE OF MEDICAL DISINFORMATION

It seems that large corporations and organizations have, in recent years, taken advantage of modern technology to keep members of the public – especially those who are making a complaint – at arm's length. It is almost impossible to reach decision makers on the telephone, and it can take months, or even years, to receive a reply to written complaints. Many requests are for information about matters that concern the claimant or complainant in important ways. Yet many organizations operate in clandestine ways, often quite outside the spirit of the law, and have, in many cases, devised complex linguistic strategies to avoid providing information that consumers need. This chapter will illustrate one such case and conclude by discussing some of the strategies used.

Case History

A patient at a large NHS (National Health Service) hospital somewhere in the United Kingdom (we will call him Mr Anthony), was attempting to get copies of his medical records because he believed that a major operation he had undergone in 2003 was unnecessary. He believed that if the surgeon who operated on him in 2003 had properly familiarized himself with his medical history, which related to an earlier operation in 1995, he would not have operated and thus caused him, Mr Anthony, further medical problems.

After a number of phone calls and letters Mr Anthony had still not received all of the information he wanted from the hospital, and – in fact – the hospital had notified him that they were not able to do any more. He then wrote to the complaints unit of the hospital to report the situation and eventually received a letter from the hospital chief executive which exonerated the hospital of any blame.

The paper trail certainly seemed to indicate several inconsistencies. In a letter of 22 April 2003 the hospital chief executive wrote advising Mr Anthony that he had already received his complete medical records.

However, according to Mr Anthony the records he had received contained no mention of the 1995 operation. He wrote to tell them this, but did not receive a reply until 16 October 2003, in which the hospital said they were writing to 'provide copies of the records you have requested'. Clearly, then, Mr Anthony could not have received his complete medical records in April. Closer examination of the April letter inadvertently appears to admit as much, because it claims 'we advised that you had received copies of your medical notes . . . *in accordance with your request.*' This suggests that there may have been certain records that Mr Anthony was not aware of, and that the hospital was adhering strictly to his non-technical request, in which he would quite probably have failed to request certain records, perhaps because he did not know all of the records which were held – hence 'in accordance with your request'.

Quite often when large corporate organizations deal with private individuals, they are able to use apparently innocuous phrases like 'in accordance with your request' to deny access to information which may not have been in the letter of Mr Anthony's request, but which a reasonable person would have interpreted as having been intended by Mr Anthony. This happens because most complainants are ordinary citizens with no technical knowledge of how large organizations work, of how records are kept, and indeed have little concept of the bureaucratic machinery with which they are dealing. Furthermore, it seems from the April letter that the chief executive is distinguishing between *records* and *notes*, a distinction Mr Anthony may not have entertained as being significant. Although in some cases the distinction between 'medical records' and 'medical notes' may be significant, it could be that – in order to avoid releasing certain types of documentation – the chief executive was exploiting this possible lack of conceptual clarity on Mr Anthony's part to claim that all requests had been acceded to. However, although the phrase 'medical notes' appears innocuous and non-technical, if used in this way – as a type of documentation to be distinguished from 'medical records' – it is clear the chief executive is using the phrase technically, and possibly as a way of denying Mr Anthony information contained in the *records* rather than the *notes*.

Professionals working within such organizations know that they can protect the activities of their organization with such linguistic strategies. When the chief executive says, also in the April letter, that 'We also advised that there were other records relating to treatment in 1995. . . . not disclosed . . . because you did not request them . . .', this sounds disingenuous since, as it turns out, the treatment Mr Anthony had in 2000 was linked, medically and historically, to the treatment he had had in 1995, and therefore the earlier records were germane to his quest for information. The use of the verb to *disclose* is interesting in this context – '. . . these [records] were not disclosed . . .' – because to *disclose a record* is a much less frequent use of the word to *disclose* than to *disclose information*. An internet search reveals that the latter usage is nearly 60 times more common than the former.[1]

Using a professional language corpus (Cobuild) I discovered that 'information' is in fact the most frequent collocate of 'disclose'. There were no instances of 'records' with 'disclose'. It is also noticeable that the sentence which includes the use of the word 'disclose' is in the passive, namely, 'these were not disclosed'. The sentence does not say by whom the records were not disclosed – this is known as an *agentless passive*. Using an agentless passive enables the writer, the chief executive, to distance himself from that which was not 'disclosed'. Moreover, since 'disclose' is much more common when used with 'information' it suggests that the chief executive knows that there has been a failure to 'disclose' information. By using the passive, especially an agentless passive, he is able to distance himself from the process. This is also evident in other phrases used by the chief executive in the April letter, for example: 'I understand that you have not made reference to any other records.' This implies that the writer does not know for sure, only that he 'understands', probably through a third party. A similar note is struck with 'I was sorry to learn that you are unable to accept my findings.' This suggests that the chief executive did not 'learn' this direct from Mr Anthony, but from someone else. All of these instances point to the chief executive attempting to distance himself from Mr Anthony's complaint. In his closing sentence the chief executive says 'Regrettably, in the circumstances I must conclude that there is nothing further we can add which might help resolve this matter to your satisfaction.' This suggests further distancing strategies, for example, 'I must conclude' implies that the writer has done everything in his power, but this is partly contradicted by 'nothing . . . we can add which might help resolve this matter', which implies that the chief executive does not know exactly what will resolve the matter. However, Mr Anthony has been very specific about what would resolve the matter: full sight of his records.

In the letter of 8 October, the chief executive writes: '. . . Mr Smith, Chief Consultant, whom as you know chaired the Local Resolution Meeting and has been absent on leave . . . on his return we shall look further into your comments'.

I wondered why the writer says he has been *'absent* on leave'. 'On leave' implies that the person being referred to *is absent*. It could of course be that he 'has been' on leave, has finished his leave, but is still officially 'absent'. This suggests that the writer might not wish to state that the Chief Consultant is actually available for discussion, and could therefore be a device for delaying the access to Mr Anthony's records which, in any case, become available by the time the letter of the 16 October is written by the chief executive, scarcely more than a week later.

Mr Anthony also requested a copy of the video tape of the 'Local Resolution Meeting' because he felt this tape contained important information about his treatment. Referring to the video tape the chief executive states that the purpose of the tape was to facilitate the preparation of notes of the meeting, and that thereafter the tapes would be wiped.

He actually says: 'Once this material has been completed then practice is for the tapes to be wiped and reused.' The chief executive does not state that the tapes were actually wiped, just that it is the practice to do so. In fact he does not say it is 'the practice', but that 'practice is'. As with *absent* on leave', which we discussed earlier, there is some redundancy in the phrase 'wiped and reused'. Why would the tapes be 'wiped' if they were going to be 'reused'?

Finally on this point, why does the writer then add 'Regrettably, we are unable to provide you with copies of the tapes'? He has already implied this. This could indicate that the tapes, or copies of them, do exist. I offer this suggestion because of an interesting area of linguistics referred to as *Grice's Conversational Maxims*. This curious sounding theory considers the issue of 'how much' information speakers/writers give and what the quality of that information is. At an informal level it seems to me, regarding the tapes, that the Chief Executive is protesting a little too much (quantity) while the 'quality' aspect also seems poor: 'Once this material has been completed then practice is for the tapes to be wiped and reused. Regrettably, we are unable to provide you with copies of the tapes'. Here I would have expected the Chief Executive to begin with his regret, followed by the explanation, for example 'Unfortunately we cannot provide you with copies of the tapes because they have been re-used, as is our practice'. Informally, it seems to me that the Chief Executive is weighing his words with a little too much care.

However, we can see that Mr Anthony has still not received all of his records, because in the 16 October letter the chief executive says: '. . . I am advised [by whom? In what context?] that you have now had full access to all documents that are applicable under the given circumstances'. This indicates that there are still records which Mr Anthony has not received, only those that are 'applicable'. Doubtless there is a hospital or National Health Service guideline about what is applicable under what circumstances – but how would Mr Anthony know this? The chief executive's words indicates that there may be records which are not being given to Mr Anthony, because they are not documents that conform to the 'given circumstances'. However, he does not state what these documents are, nor what the circumstances are nor, crucially, how Mr Anthony could find out how to obtain any documents he does not already have.

Moreover, the excerpt 'Your request for other records in any physical, electronic or other forms as permitted by the Data Protection Act has been addressed . . .' could be taken to mean that the Data Protection Act restricts, in Mr Anthony's case under 'given circumstances', access to certain records, when in fact the sentence – as I read it – seems to mean nothing more than that the Data Protection Act restricts the forms which records may take (physical, electronic etc). By then coupling this with '. . . I am now advised that you have had full access to all documents that are applicable under the given circumstances' the reader could be forgiven for thinking that there are restrictions under the Data Protection Act and that the writer is claiming he is following the Data Protection Act, and is in fact mandated by it to restrict access to further records.

There was little doubt that Mr Anthony had suffered delay and prevarication at the hands of the Chief Executive of the hospital concerned, who through his use of language appears to have employed stratagems designed to obscure the truth as to what Mr Anthony was entitled to know, and which records he was entitled to view, and thereby avoiding a timely resolution to vital matters relating to Mr Anthony's health and well-being. At the very least the organization lacked transparency. Large organizations have the ability to hide behind rules, regulations and procedures which are opaque to the lay person. Even the process of communicating with them is made difficult by modern technology (e.g. telephone systems with a confusing array of input options 'If you want X please press 1, 2, 3' etc). Organizations can obfuscate, delay, confuse, resort to technical language which sounds like everyday language, and generally play the corporate game with little fear of being brought to account. Fortunately, close linguistic analysis can reveal the kinds of linguistic strategy in use by some corporations. In the present instance the strategy appears to be fourfold: to (i) use common language which is also technical language in the context of the organization's activities; (ii) imply, by ambiguity, that there is legislation which controls or restricts the kinds of information to which the consumer is entitled; (iii) employ definitional categories using semantic terms with which the consumer is unfamiliar and (iv) avoid an implied meaning by resorting to literal terminology. These strategies are tabulated in Table 10.1.

Common linguistic techniques to achieve the above strategic aims include the use of the following: lexical and clausal ambiguity partly by exploiting polysemy, agentless passive constructions, long sentences consisting of multiple clauses often with deferred verbs or objects and clauses

Table 10.1. List of strategies to achieve non-informational ends

Linguistic device	Example	Comment
Uses common language which is also technical	'notes', 'records': is there a difference?	The hospital is able to exploit a semantic distinction which the consumer may not know about.
Implication that legislation restricts the permitted response	'Your request for other records in . . . other forms as permitted by the Data Protection Act has been addressed . . .'	The Data Protection Act is designed to protect the consumer – yet here we have an ambiguity that suggests the 'request' is permitted by the Act, rather than the form in which the record is being held. Legislation is being invoked to restrict what the consumer is entitled to know about *him*self.
Employ definitional categories using semantic terms with which the consumer is unfamiliar	'I am now advised that you have had full access to all documents that are applicable under the given circumstances . . .'	What kind of documents are applicable under what circumstances? How would Mr Anthony necessarily know what those circumstances are. Hence 'applicable' and 'given circumstances' are being used to illustrate categories of which Mr Anthony is not aware.
Avoid an implied meaning by resorting to literal terminology	'. . . in accordance with your request'	Here the hospital is taking Mr Anthony's request literally, yet knowing that there are technical senses in which he has used words which he takes to have only an ordinary meaning in the context.

with 'fuzzy' scope. Clearly the hospital has violated all the basic precepts of plain English usage and has used linguistic means to achieve what can only be termed as institutional abuse.

Mr Anthony pursued the hospital trust to court and, at the last minute, the hospital agreed a settlement with him. Hopefully, forensic linguistics played a small part in this procedure.

Note

1. Internet search on Google on 27 May 2008 showed: 'disclose a record' 30,100; 'disclose information' 1,720,000.

Reference

Grice, P. (1975). 'Logic and Conversation'. In Cole and Morgan (1975), pp. 41–58.

11

STRATEGIES FOR CODE: A PRISONER'S DILEMMA

What kinds of strategies do people use when they are determined to commit a crime but have to keep it secret from others? Most professional criminals know how to keep quiet and so this does not usually apply, but when the crime being committed involves language, then it is not so easy.

About 8 years ago a man was serving a sentence at a prison somewhere in the United Kingdom for sexual offences with a child, whom I shall call 'X'. I cannot give any identifying information about Mr Aberthenot, as I shall call him, because it is important the identity of his victim remains concealed. While in prison Mr Aberthenot wrote frequent letters to X, who was then aged 13. To keep his correspondence secret, he devised a number of linguistic strategies. To begin with, he hit on the idea of addressing the letters, not to X herself, but to an actual friend of his, whom I shall call Mike, and although this was surprisingly effective at first he must have suspected that it would not be long before someone – other than X herself – would read beyond 'Dear Mike' or 'Hello Mate' and so would realize who the real recipient of the letters was. Moreover, the replies he was getting from X started to become increasingly explicit and to demand explicit replies in return. Prisoners all over the world are familiar with the process of communicating with each other secretly, and according to Mayr (2004),[1] the use of codes in prisoner language is probably universal. But the letter writer who is trying to conceal an offence from the censorship authorities has a different motivation from the ordinary prisoner who simply wishes to exhibit resistance or is perhaps showing solidarity with other inmates.

The clandestine letter writer in prison needs to make sure that what he writes will not be clear to any reader other than his intended audience because, if found out, he could face severe penalties, including an extended prison term. But Mr Aberthenot's overwhelming desire to retain sexual control of his victim caused him to take dangerous risks with his freedom: it seemed he would do anything to continue conducting the sexual relationship remotely.

The first hint of a code comes in a letter from X herself. Replying, Mr Aberthenot is at first bemused: 'What you on about that slang stuff?' he writes. Then, a little further down the page the penny suddenly seems to drop and he begins to reply in code. The code used by X is Pig Latin, made famous by the television series, *The Simpsons*. It is a very easy code to learn. In order to disguise a word, the first letter of the word is removed, placed at the end of the word, and followed by an invented, constant, suffix, namely '-ay'. Thus, the word 'say' first has the 's' repositioned at the end of the word, giving 'ays'. This is then followed by the '-ay' suffix, producing 'aysay' for 'say'. So, 'happy birthday' for example becomes, in Pig Latin 'appyhay irthdaybay'. With some words the task is not as straightforward, for example the word 'I' has only one letter, and so no repositioning can take place – it therefore becomes just 'Iay'. The word 'you' is also awkward, and would be rendered 'ouyay' if the formula were followed exactly. To simplify matters, Pig Latinists often use 'eway' instead of 'ouyay'. Similarly, 'to' is often rendered as 'ewtay'.

The Aberthenot letters contain many examples in Pig Latin, including 'Iay ishway Iay asway akingway upay extnay ewtay eway everyay ayday'. This reads as 'I wish I was waking up next to you every day'. The letters were always nominally addressed to 'Dear Mike', but it was apparent that unless Mr Aberthenot was saying that he wished to wake up next to 'Mike' every day, then it was clear that the actual addressee – as opposed to the nominal addressee – was not 'Mike' but someone else.

A devotee of music, Mr Aberthenot had always made plenty of references to his favourite songs – all love songs – in his letters. He actually used this to help disguise the fact that he was using code at all. So, for example, he would write: 'I've got a tune for you'. This mention of a 'tune' would then be followed by the coded text. In addition, he sometimes referred to the 'tune' after having presented the coded text, for instance by saying: 'Did you like that tune?' or words to that effect. This would mean that anyone glossing the letters casually might have assumed that the coded part of the text was a lyric of some kind. Given the resistance of our brains to unfamiliar language forms, whether spoken or on paper, the presence of the code might ironically actually have deterred anyone from inspecting the letters too closely. In fact, unless anyone reading the letters had been interested in the same kind of music as Mr Aberthenot himself, they would most likely have glossed over that part of the text without a second thought, but of course the messages were not tunes at all. They were highly explicit descriptions of Mr Aberthenot's fantasies.

After a time Mr Aberthenot must have begun to realize that Pig Latin might be a bit too easy to decipher, and so he developed a new code. This consisted of an invented prefix 'glob' followed by the word to be encoded minus the first letter. Hence 'love', for example, might be written 'globove'. However, in common with many creators of SMS texting on mobile phones and other computer media, he often used simplified spellings, and so 'love' was usually written 'luv', rendering 'globuv' for 'love' rather than 'globove'. Hence 'I love you' is written 'globi globuv globu', which is in reality 'I luv u'. As with Pig Latin, when we have to encode single-letter words, for example, 'I', the word is given in full after the prefix. Thus the 'glob' code is really a variant of the Pig Latin code. Whereas Pig Latin moves the first letter of the word to the end of the word and then adds a constant suffix '-ay', the 'glob' code begins with a constant prefix, 'glob', and omits the first letter altogether (if there is more than one letter in the word). It is therefore quite easy to encode in Glob, and only slightly more difficult to decode glob than it is to decode Pig Latin. Any constant prefix or suffix can be used in either case. It just happens that Glob uses 'glob' and Pig Latin uses 'ay'. Also, in either case what is presented as a suffix could have been presented as a prefix, and vice versa.

In some cases in Glob, there is a possible ambiguity as to which word is intended, for example the phrase '. . . globat globime globot globastin globi globime globuvin globu' has two instances of 'globime'. Since they occupy positions near to each other, thus suggesting different grammatical rôles and therefore meanings, this could lead to ambiguity. Decoding the easiest words first, we get 'globat globime **not** globastin globi globime **luvin u**'. From this we see that the first 'globime' appears before the negative particle 'not' leading us to assume that it might be a pronoun followed by an auxiliary verb in contracted form, in this case apparently 'I'm' but written 'Ime'. This would imply that the word after 'not', 'globastin', is the continuous participle of a verb, that is, the head word[2] of a verb + 'ing' (here shortened to 'in-'), in this case 'wasting'. This leads us to believe that what follows the pronoun+auxiliary+negative particle+verb construction is a grammatical object, and if we assume that 'i' is actually 'my' (spelled 'mi') with the 'm' removed, then it follows that the word after 'my' is likely to be a noun. This four letter noun ends in the letters 'ime', so 'time' appears to be the most appropriate from the possible set of words that meet the criteria of a word which is four letters long, the last three letters of which are '-ime', namely (dime, lime, mime, time). The word 'time' is a frequent collocate of the verb 'wasting' or 'wastin-' so the phrase is likely to be 'that I'm not wasting my time loving you'. Another way to decode 'glob' is to remove the prefix, leaving 'at ime ot astin i ime uvin u'. If read or spoken aloud this has the effect of placing a glottal[3] stop at the beginning of each word, which can then easily be substituted for an appropriate phoneme, since one can often recognize a word according to its prosody (intonation) and without knowledge of its first phoneme (especially if this is not a vowel). If the general phonetic shape of an individual word is of no help, we can often look to the overall prosody of the phrase for clues to interpretation. As the reader can see, this code is relatively easy to break, allowing for the occasional ambiguity, which – however – is usually resolved by grammatical context or neighbouring content.

Even using Glob, one difficulty Mr Aberthenot had was how to reference X in the letters. Sometimes when referring to X by name, he would put the entire name in lower case. It would therefore be possible that the casual reader might miss this reference since proper names are harder to notice if there is no initial upper-case letter. At a particular point in time, however, Mr Aberthenot apparently realized the risks of naming the child and from then on contrived to avoid referring to her by her actual name. Having said this, he was certainly very careless in the early days of their correspondence to have mentioned her name at all – or maybe he was simply over-confident in his luck or his abilities.

So, once he stopped using her actual name, Mr Aberthenot began to refer to X in the third person. Thus, we began to get references such as 'your kid', 'the one you know about', 'you know who' and so on. Given that he was ostensibly writing to 'Mike', but was actually writing to X this could make comprehension difficult on occasion. Because of the need to keep up the pretence that he was writing to 'Mike', Mr Aberthenot devised further tactics, including the following:

- Swearing: Mr Aberthenot often used swearing or 'bad language' in his letters. Although in modern society, especially among the under-40 age group, swearing is as common among females as it is among males (see Holliday et al., 2004: 18),[4] probably its main use in such contexts is as a bonding mechanism with same-gender interactants. Examples in Aberthenot–Mike's letters include: 'you're right about that prick'; 'Quit taking the piss out of the job . . .'; 'made me piss my sides . . .' and 'Just wanted to smash the **** out of all those muppets . . . no **** else wants to know' (also 2/11/05). It seemed that by swearing and making derogatory remarks about other males any casual reader might have been led to view the letters as being typical of 'male talk', and would therefore have been less alert to content of an intimate nature which was interspersed within the 'male talk';

- References to alcohol: There are a number of references to alcohol. These appear to be intended to foster the stereotype of males drinking together. Examples include: 'Please don't write about going on the piss next time, I'd love a beer right now . . .'; '. . . a pint would be lovely right now'; 'Done it again, didn't you! Going on about booze and pubs. I'd love one right now';
- Use of 'mate': Depending on the context, males often use the word 'mate' as a way of bonding with other males. Examples include 'Hope you enjoy your hols mate.'

Further, male bonding was encoded in expressions of loyalty, with the writer stating he was able to 'count on' the addressee. Examples included 'Still got some friends out there and I know I could count on you', and 'As I said in my last letter I know I can count on you mate'. In some letters the task of multi-addressing begins to tell on Mr Aberthenot's concentration and the pretence that 'you' is 'she' starts to unravel. So, for example, he begins one letter addressed to 'Mike', but ends the first paragraph with 'she': 'Said this before but you are the only one who really does know me and I meant that as well, I would go to the ends of the earth + back as long as she was happy mate'. In this instance the writer appears to have forgotten that he used 'you' in the first half of the sentence and subsequently talks about 'she'. The other possibility is that Mr Aberthenot was hoping that any official who read the letter might be lazy and focus mainly on the first part of the sentence. In long sentences with a number of pronouns or other references it can be quite easy to become disoriented and forget who the subject was by the time you get to the end of the sentence.

A similar phenomenon occurs in a later letter where Mr Aberthenot refers to a fight he had with two other prisoners and then says '. . . bet Xs gina (i.e. 'going to') be mad with me?' In his next letter he says 'Knew you'd be mad at that letter'. Since this is the only reference, in these two letters, to his addressee being 'mad' at/with him, it seems Mr Aberthenot has forgotten that he is supposed to be giving the impression of addressing his nominal addressee and not his actual addressee. He therefore addresses 'X' as 'you' rather than 'she'.

There were many references to sexual matters in the letters, including some very graphic descriptions. However, I shall confine myself to the apparently more innocuous ones here: 'Wasn't lying when I said I've not had sex since March 98, you should know what I'm like, it has to be with the right person'. Was this really addressed to Mike? Mr Aberthenot also says: 'God if I was out tomorrow you know who I'd go to see first no doubt about that, mind you I might have forgot what to do.' In this excerpt we see that Mr Aberthenot seems to consider himself in a sexual relationship with someone, that he is 'saving' himself for this person, and that he longs to visit this person for sexual purposes.

Once the letters had been decoded and the various linguistic strategies uncovered, Mr Aberthenot was interviewed by officers at the prison. Without forewarning him about the letters the detective in the case began by suggesting that he, Mr Aberthenot, had a sexual interest in Mike. Mr Aberthenot hotly denied this. The detective then said: 'But surely you want to wake up next to Mike every day?' He quoted from another letter: 'globi globant globait ewtay globiss globu globon your ----'.[5] The detective asked: 'So, where exactly is it that you would like to kiss Mike then?' Given that Mike was 47, weighed about 18 stone and did not routinely wash or shave, there is little doubt the detective was being mischievous. Mr Aberthenot had been outmanoeuvred.

Notes

1. Mayr, Andrea (2004). *Prison Discourse. Language as a Means of Control and Resistance.* New York: Palgrave Macmillan.
2. The 'head word' is the form of the word found in the dictionary.
3. The kind of sound speakers of certain English dialects produce when saying, for example, 'butter'. If the 't' sound is removed a 'glottal stop' is produced.
4. Holliday, A., M. Hyde and J. Kullman (2004). *Intercultural Communication: An Advanced Resource Book.* New York: Routledge.
5. 'I can't wait to kiss you on your ----'.

12

A GENOCIDE IN RWANDA

Many readers will recall that in 1994, the central African country of Rwanda played host to the horror of a genocide, when nearly a million people were massacred in the space of just a few months. Most of the victims were members of the Tutsi ethnic group. The world seemed powerless to prevent the slaughter of men, women and children. Many of the perpetrators were government officials who subsequently escaped to Europe, including the United Kingdom.

In the course of time the Rwandan government compiled a list of suspects, obtained witness statements from former victims and others, and began requesting European governments to extradite the genocide suspects back to Rwanda. One of these was a Mr U, then living in the United Kingdom. The issue for the forensic linguist, as always, is not whether the defendant is guilty or not of a particular crime, but what the standard of evidence is when evaluated linguistically. Primarily this means: what is the linguistic quality of the evidence? Is it independent, accurate, impartially obtained? Is the statement an eye-witness account or is it hearsay? Does the statement attempt to reproduce the spoken words of the witness, or does it appear to have been altered? Does the statement contain actual observation or just opinion?

To be truthful, I have no idea whether Mr U, a Hutu from Rwanda, and one-time mayor (burgomaster) of K in Rwanda, ordered and participated in the killings of his neighbours and friends, the Tutsis of his commune in 1994. He may have done. On the other hand, he may be completely innocent. All I can comment on is the status of the linguistic evidence presented against him, in particular the many witness statements received by the Home Office in the United Kingdom from the authorities in Rwanda.

The statements were in French when received by the Home Office and I was immediately concerned that the translation quality was very poor. Translators are conscientious people. Normally, the Home Office employs only the best translators and it is rare to find a serious mistake.

One of the statements, in French, was as follows:

Une semaine après notre arrivée (13 avril), nous avons appris que des militaires de la Garde Présidentielle étaient arrivés a K où ils ont commencé à tuer les Tutsi.

Dès le lendemain, nous avons appris que des Interahamwe, accompagnés d'éléments de la Garde Présidentielle sont arrivés à la Commune où ils seront entretenus avec le Bourgmestre (U) et l'Assistant Bourgmestre.

The Home Office translation of this document was as follows:

A week after our arrival (13 April) we learned that militia of the presidential guard had arrived at K where they began killing Tutsis.

The next day, we learned that Interahamwe, accompanied by members of the presidential guard, had arrived at the commune where they were supported by the Mayor (U) and the Assistant Mayor.

Aside from observing that the writer of the original French document was probably not a native speaker of French, the underlined section above also gave me cause for concern: '. . . they were supported . . .' In fact, the French version 'ils seront entretenus' means 'they were said to have had discussions with' and not 'they were supported'. It is a completely different meaning. The translation, as given by the Home Office translator, was just plain wrong. Either the Home Office translator had entered the task with a high degree of personal or political prejudice, or had simply made an error, or was totally incompetent.

The fact that the writer of the statements was not a native speaker also worried me: had the statements been translated from Kinyarwandan by a local Kinyarwanda native speaker, or had they been taken down in French by a Kinyarwanda speaker? The former seemed more likely, with a later translation ensuing. Moreover, some of the statements were incomplete, sometimes beginning with dots, namely, '. . . after the death of President Habyarima' for example. They also showed other signs of editing. Clearly, the statements had suffered editorialization from several hands – for example, there were requests – in French – for further information. It seemed, on balance, therefore, that the scribe was likely to be a native Kinyarwandan speaker who was being asked to interview witnesses by a French native speaker. The Rwandan person then noted down the answers in Rwandan, later translating them into French. The native French speaker then probably edited the translation.

In itself such a procedure would not automatically disqualify the statements as reliable, independent accounts of what witnesses saw. But anyone taking statements in such a context as the aftermath of a major event such as a genocide should be transparent, stating plainly who had taken the statements, in what language, when and by whom they had been translated, if there had been further editorial supervision, and so on.

In addition, the statements showed very little sign of spoken language, and heavy signs of 'writtenness'. Somewhere, within those statements, was the language of the original speakers – but how accurate was the transition from speech into writing – and, furthermore, the translation across several languages? Also, given that none of the statements bore the names of the witnesses – possibly for reasons of personal safety – there was no way of testing any of the statements for accuracy. There is another issue. The person taking the statements was probably someone in authority, certainly of higher authority than the witnesses. It is very easy to influence people when you are in a position of authority. We can also ask ourselves whether Mr U was perhaps known to the person taking the statements, and whether this individual may have had some personal or political *animus* towards Mr U.

There seemed to me to be several indications of hearsay in the statements. For example one statement read:

> Two weeks after [the president's] death . . . U held an awareness raising meeting . . . After this meeting the Interahamwe, assisted by the authorities, set about killing . . . Tutsi[s].

The witness does not state that s/he attended this meeting, nor how s/he knew who was at that meeting. Linking the killing of Tutsis to 'after this meeting' implies a connection which may be no more than temporal – but is here given as causal. This excerpt raises a number of other linguistic issues, for example: What does 'assisted by the authorities' mean? How does the witness know that the Interahamwe were 'assisted'? Which authorities? This excerpt condenses a lot of information into a small number of words. It strongly suggests that the witness had been asked a series of questions, that the answers to these questions were then written down, and that the whole was later condensed into a compact re-phrasing of what was originally said.

The same witness also states: 'I remember the case of the late Beatrice who was raped then killed'. I suggest that the word 'remember' means the witness may not have seen either the raping or killing, and thus this account could be construed as hearsay.

In another statement we have: 'Other local leaders agreed to collaborate with Callixte in the massacres against the Tutsis . . . namely *Charles U*'. As before, I suggest this statement relies on hearsay, or at least does not make specific the source of information. The degree of grammatical elaboration and the complexity of the vocabulary both suggest a written rather than a spoken medium, possibly in a question and answer format. The word 'agree' is particularly fraught with dangers in the criminal context ('accepter' in the French). What does 'agree' really mean? How does the witness know that this agreement took place, and what its form was?

Yet another statement begins: 'I attended that meeting . . . which was announced over loudspeakers to be held at Progress Building.' It is unclear from this whether this text was edited because the witness begins 'I attended *that* meeting'. In this case *that* could be a reference to something which was previously said but is not recorded here, or it could mean that this was a meeting known to have been announced over loudspeakers. There is another possibility – that the person giving this statement was with other people when the statement was given. One of them may have referred to the meeting in question, at which point this witness says: 'I attended *that* meeting . . .' If statements were taken in groups then this further calls into question their independence and autonomy from each other.

Gradually, as I went through the statements I found more and more examples of hearsay. For example: 'They were saying that they had received the order from the burgomaster to kill . . .' Several of the witnesses' names – as with other statements – are blanked out, and the people who are reported as saying that they had received this order are not mentioned by name. In the same statement the witness says,[1] with reference to several people who saw themselves as potential victims: 'The persons concerned, wanting to flee, first of all asked the advice of the burgomaster who reassured them, telling them . . .' This too appears to be hearsay since we are not told if the witness heard or saw this for him/herself. There is no indication that this was witnessed first-hand. Further, there is in this statement, at the beginning of the last paragraph, a series of dots (. . .) indicating the possibility that something was edited from this statement. It is not immediately clear that this paragraph is connected with the previous text in the statement.

It became apparent that some of the statements resembled each other, perhaps more closely than would have occurred had the statements been produced entirely independently of each other. For example, consider the two quotations below:

- 'During the genocide, the burgomaster had requisitioned the ambulance from the health service, used to transport the staff to work. He put the ambulance to use in the genocide operation.'
- 'During the genocide, the ambulance which was transporting us was requisitioned by the burgomaster in order to transport members of the Interahamwe and to drive around the districts of K.'

Given that these two statements were taken on the same day, and given previous remarks about the possibility that statements were taken in groups, it is possible that the two witnesses may have been giving their statement at least within each other's hearing. This similarity between the two statements raises doubts about the reliability of their content.

In addition to signs of hearsay many of the statements appear to give an opinion, rather than actual evidence. For example we have a number of examples which appear to speculate about what U, the mayor (or burgomaster) knew, such as: 'I am convinced that this incident did not escape the attention of the burgomaster'; The burgomaster . . . could not be ignorant about the existence of . . .'; 'The burgomaster could not help noticing . . .' These examples led me to think that witnesses had been asked specific questions, such as 'Did the burgomaster know', or 'Did you think the burgomaster had noticed . . .' and so on. In a court of law, questions of this nature would be regarded as leading or having the potential to lead a witness. Certainly, the witnesses appear to be giving their opinion regarding what the burgomaster may or may not have known. Witnesses, other than expert witnesses, should not give their opinion, but should report on what they personally observed or knew to be the case.

In one statement the word *rumour* crops up: 'It was thus that the rumour [of machetes at the home of X] was hawked around the place until it reached the ears of the burgomaster. He organised a meeting in the market-place at B. I don't know the exact date of this meeting. . . . Speaking publicly, Mr U . . . spoke, addressing himself to X . . . "set up barriers so that the Tutsi's don't escape you".'

The word 'rumour' here is troubling. How do we know that the burgomaster organized the meeting as a result of this rumour if he 'organised' it at all? What does 'organised' mean? The witness does not state that s/he attended this meeting. This statement, like several others has (. . .) in it, indicating cuts and possible edits.

On the above basis I felt strongly that the case against Mr U had not been well documented. Statements should be transparent, not only as to their content, but also as to their means of production. It should be clear when a witness is speculating or relying on hearsay. It should also be clear when an opinion is being given in answer to a specific question, or whether the opinion is being given spontaneously. When questions are asked, they should be recorded in the statement. Preferably, the entire interaction should be videoed or audio-recorded. I felt, on balance, that the linguistic aspect of the evidence against Mr U was poor.

At his Asylum and Immigration Tribunal hearing the judges ruled that the above linguistic objections did not constitute sufficient grounds for reversing the Home Office's decision to refuse Mr U the right to stay in the United Kingdom. The Home Office had only to show that there were 'serious reasons' to believe that Mr U had committed acts of genocide. This is a much lower level of proof than either 'on the balance of probabilities' or 'beyond reasonable doubt'.

I believe that since his asylum tribunal hearing Mr U has been deported back to Rwanda where he now faces charges of genocide. Is he guilty? On the basis of the above statements it is not possible to say. In any case this is not a question forensic linguists are employed to answer. However, it is certain that the linguistic quality of the statements is very poor.

Note

1. I am writing 'says' here for brevity sake, but I actually mean 'is alleged to have said'. This applies to similar constructions in my commentary on some of the other statements.

13

DEATH THREATS IN THE TROPICS

I have a confession to make. The case I am about to relate to you has always left me puzzled and uncomfortable. It is one of those cases where the result is necessarily tentative, where one can never be quite sure. This is why I am giving the texts below almost in their entirety. I am simply presenting them for your consideration. This is not because I believe this case offers any startling discoveries or any dramatic developments. On the contrary, I offer it as an example of a not uncommon situation in forensic work, where – despite popular belief – there are occasions where the forensic scientist is moving in uncharted waters. However, I am confident that one of my readers, somewhere, will perhaps see something in these texts that I missed.

The case concerned the deputy manager of a charitable organization working in the tropics. Of Russian descent, Boris Oblomov (not his real name) had grown up in the United Kingdom, attended agricultural college and soon after graduating went to work in India on UN food programmes. He soon developed a flair for agriculture in under-developed countries, especially in the area of animal husbandry. After a number of years in Asia he moved to another country in the tropics.

While some people may imagine that voluntary organization workers have a luxurious time out in the sun-soaked spots of the world, life is in fact quite hard for most of them. Things are certainly more complicated than having to attend an office for a few hours a day, sign a couple of cheques and then head for the beach. Some of these workers genuinely risk their lives to bring aid and assistance to people in poorer countries, and can be at the mercy of corrupt officials who care nothing for the plight of the people whom the NGO workers have been sent to assist. Indeed many NGO workers have been arrested on the slightest pretext and a number of them have been threatened with confiscation of their property, abduction of their relatives or even loss of life.

Such was the case with Mr Oblomov. He was now working in a country far from home where his task was to set up agricultural courses to bring about long-term improvements in farming knowledge. He had not been in the country long when he received the following email:

Text 1: First anonymous email

Mr oblomov

this is to secretely disclose to you that a group of people have been meeting in a bar in town planning how to kill you. some of them seemed to have worked for your company but leftsometimes back. They are are six, 3 of tthem look (tribe name). one person (a [tribe name]) is a very well known hitman and operates in [town name]. They were planning to abduct you on your way to airport but you left a day or two earlier. They wanted to intersept you near [place name] and take you to [place name] plantations, you would never be seen again. They all have your photos. They kknew you were going to use either a landrover, a bMw or a red honda. they are cordinating using mobiles. i dont know why they are after your life but they look very determined. now they are waitng for you to return and get you, they even know the date you want to come and want to catch you from airport. somebody in your company is helping them with details.i got to know about this as i sat in a near table and one of them forgot some papers with details behind, they wer talking without fear and looked abit drank. I sat just behind them for about 30 minitesbut did not fear at all. they were also saying that the job will cost 20,000 and any money they find with you is theirs. i advise you stay away, i do not know you but want to help you.these are real killers.

A short while later Mr Oblomov received a second email:

Text 2: Second anonymous email

Boris

I am one of the 4 employees still in the office. I have withheld my identity because I have realised that nothing is a secret any more, the author of the anonymous doc is now a public information. I write as a matter of genuine concern.

We in the office are convinced that there is a real threat at your life, some mysterious people are looking for you (different people at different times).They are not genuine people. The cops are also looking for you, they say they want to return you to court, they look like there is more than meets the eye or more that we know of.

regards

Just prior to the receipt of these emails Mr Oblomov had fallen out with the organization's secretary. Suspecting that the anonymous emails might have come from this gentleman, Mr Gonzalez, Oblomov sent several colleagues to go and see him and deliver a letter outlining his concerns. This was the reply Oblomov received (excerpt):

Text 3: Letter from former employee

First, as I informed them, I wish to also inform you that I HAVE NOTHING against you, you stated that you have been receiving threatening text messages and e-mails, I felt very sorry about this. May I bring to your attention that I have received similar messages which are probably worse, I shared those messages with the team and they were shocked, they are still in my mobile and I will show them to you. I have also received e-mail messages, which would move you to tears if you read them. I personally have no time to sit and write such messages at all, they depict a person of very low mental caliber. If I have anything to tell you, I would write to you directly and would never hide my identity, however bitter that message might be. I showed the team the only SMS that I ever wrote directly to you and I did it in good faith, I am sorry if it hurt you, it was never my intention to do so. All of us came to a conclusion that somebody or some people are sitting between us and fuelling the whole matter; they probably want to destroy the organization. It's important therefore that you investigate the source of that information, inform the police and beef up your personal security, please do not risk with your life.

Finally, I ask you to prevail upon the author of the document to come public, at least to reveal himself to you, he or she would then clarify some of the issues to you and therefore you would be in a better position to discuss them out with me. Lets remain positive and remove the perception of hostility or enemity, between you and me, its not there.

Thank you

PW Gonzalez

One of the first observations I would make is that there are a number of references to 'your life' in these texts, each preceded by a different preposition. Thus, in the two questioned documents we have 'i dont know why they are *after* your life but they look very determined' and 'we in the office are convinced that there is a real threat *at* your life', while in the known text we have 'beef up your personal security, please do not risk *with* your life'. This is not necessarily anything to do with authorship, but it is nevertheless interesting in the light of quite competent preposition usage elsewhere in the texts. Preposition usage is one of the hardest things for non-native speakers to master. Another aspect of English difficult to absorb for many learners is the use of 'the'. For the most part the texts reveal fairly competent usage of 'the', with some errors, for example 'to airport' and 'from airport' instead of 'to the airport' and 'from the airport'. However, the lexico-grammar[1] is very competent: we find words like 'intercept', 'concern', 'determined', 'withheld' and 'convinced' used without difficulty. Hence, seeing 'i' in lower case (several times), and 'were' spelled as 'wer' does not convince me that the writer lacks competence or basic skill. Consider also the fact that Text 1 begins with a lower case letter and that 'secretly' is spelled 'secretely', or that 'BMW' is written bMw'. Along with 'leftsometimes', 'kknew' and 'waitng' the curious capitalization of 'bMw' purports to indicate a writer who is not skilled at using a keyboard. However, what I believe is really happening is that the writer of the anonymous letters is consciously disguising his/her style and level of keyboard ability. Apparent keyboard incompetence and basic misspellings are common authorship masks. However, these efforts at demonstrating a lack of ability are contradicted by other signs of skilful use of the language – such as the examples given above. Hence, I wondered if these were really letters of 'genuine concern' as they claimed to be or that the writer really wanted 'to help you'.

Another point of interest that occurred to me was that Mr Gonzalez appears to view the apparent threats to Mr Oblomov's life purely in terms of the problems which exist between them: 'All of us came to a conclusion that somebody or some people are sitting between us and fuelling the whole matter' and 'some ex staff members have taken a great interest in this matter and I have a feeling that a possibility that they could be fuelling it cannot be ruled out'.

Again, this is not an authorship issue, but it leads me to the next point: these references to 'somebody or some people' and especially 'some ex staff members' from the Gonzalez letter appear to echo 'some of them seem to have worked for your company' from anonymous Text 1. We also notice a parallel between 'somebody in your company is helping them with details' in the same text and 'somebody leaked the information to them'. As with many anonymous letters Texts 1 and 2 are full of innuendo. Thus, we have vague phrases like 'a group of people' and 'some mysterious people' in the anonymous texts, and this is paralleled by 'somebody or some people' in the known letter by Mr Gonzalez. It is also noticeable that both in the questioned and known texts it is claimed that a single person is leaking the information, and more than one person – former staff members – who are doing the plotting or are involved in it.

When considering a series of anonymous texts it is important not to assume that they are necessarily from the same author. The links I found of interest between the two anonymous texts were the references to 'people' previously mentioned, the apparently incompetent use of the preposition with 'life', that is, 'after your life' and 'at your life', and 'real killers' compared to 'real threat'. While these are certainly not authorship markers I would not rule out that they could be indicative of common authorship.

Finally, I would draw the reader's attention to this sentence in Text 2: 'the author of the anonymous doc is now a public information'. I think what the writer means here is that it is now 'public' knowledge that Oblomov received an anonymous document. This has parallels with 'I ask you to prevail upon the author of the document to come public' in the letter by Mr Gonzalez. It is not just the fact that we have a col-location[2] between 'author', 'doc/ument' and 'public', but – crucially I believe – the way in which the word 'public' is used. In the example 'the author of the anonymous doc is now a public information' I believe that by 'public' the writer is actually referring to the people in Mr Oblomov's company – not the general public. I believe a similar interpretation may apply to the known text by Mr Gonzalez where he writes 'I ask you to prevail upon the author of the document to come public, at least to reveal himself to you'. He begins by suggesting Mr Oblomov 'prevail upon the author . . . to come public'. However, again, this does not mean that the writer should reveal his/her identity to the general public, but to Mr Oblomov or to Mr Oblomov's company, as is made clear by '. . . to reveal himself to you'. Hence, it seems that the word 'public' is being used in both texts with a very specific meaning, or at least in a very specific context.

At this point in the analysis I have to say that I have nothing to add: there certainly seem to be links between the known letter and the suspect texts, but we cannot say more than that. I certainly would not want to rule him out as a possible candidate. Unfortunately, I have not had sight of any further texts from the anonymous writer or writers as, shortly after I was commissioned to do the work, Mr Oblomov disappeared from sight. To this day I have no idea what happened to him.

Notes

1. The way in which the grammar of words is deployed. It was traditionally thought that grammar and lexis (vocabulary) were stored separately in the individual's language facility, but linguists now view the two as an integrated, inter-dependent system, with the lexicon 'selecting' a grammar. A word in our individual lexicon is thus only really part of our personal grammar when the 'rules' applicable to the word are correctly applied.
2. Collocation: literally the co-location of two words in a text. First discovered by British linguist J. R. Firth in 1951, collocations have long since formed the backbone of textual investigation in what is known as corpus linguistics.

14

FITTED UP BY A 'PROFESSIONAL':
FALSELY ACCUSED

Bill Johnson was a Midwest businessman who once enjoyed nothing more than getting into his privately owned aeroplane and flying off to Mexico to visit his holiday home. He used to be a member of a certain flying club in the Midwest, often assisting other members by flying them on pleasure trips, advising them about aircraft purchases and even helping one or two of them to build their own hangars on the grounds of the airport. Flying clubs, just like fishing clubs, chess clubs or car clubs can, however, be hotbeds of jealousy and rivalry, as groups of members vie with each other for positions on committees, better parking spots for their beloved machines, or the favour of the chairman. Bill Johnson had long since decided to keep clear of the internal politics of the club – he was just there to fly. As a highly successful contractor, with clients all over the United States he was in the fortunate position of not needing to jostle for position at the club. Mostly he flew during the weekends.

At one point in time he had been offered a plot of land on the grounds of the airport with a 25-year lease. He bought the lease and built a state of the art hangar on it. Imagine his horror when he arrived at the airport one Sunday morning to discover that his aircraft and hangar had been impounded by the owners of the flying club. He was not even allowed into the hangar to collect his personal belongings. The club's reason for this extreme step was that Johnson had been secretly authoring an internet journal which the management viewed as detrimental to their organization. They showed Johnson the internet journal they claimed he had been editing. I will refer to it as the X document. It contained articles mildly critical of the management of the flying club, but could hardly be said to be detrimental. It fact it was no more than a light-hearted, if on occasion semi-literate, look at the foibles of certain members, the vanities and ambitions of others, and the general muddle that occurs whenever you put more than ten people on a patch of earth and expect them to get along with each other. Johnson was offended because of its somewhat poor grammar, spelling and punctuation.

Protesting his innocence, Bill Johnson was told he had 'no chance'. Several club heavies escorted him to the perimeter fence and told him that not only were they going to keep his aircraft and hangar, but they were also going to sue him for every penny. They smiled gleefully as they began to describe different properties he owned, which they seemed to know quite a lot about. Growing more suspicious by the minute as to their real motives, Johnson immediately contacted his attorney to issue counter-proceedings. Realizing that they would have a fight on their hands, the club then invited a certain professor to assess whether Mr Johnson was the likely author of X. The report was duly completed and I was contacted by Mr Johnson's attorneys to see whether 'anything could be done'.

First, let me say that the professor in question is quite well known within his field, and I believe quite popular on his own campus. However, he did not appear to have a very detailed understanding of either foren-sic linguistics or authorship attribution. I could find no references to any publications of his on forensic linguistic matters or on authorship attribution, and to my knowledge he is not, nor ever has been, a member of the International Association of Forensic Linguists, which represents the academic interests of the field, publishes its own peer-reviewed jour-nal and regularly holds international conferences.

This lack of experience began to show at an early stage. For example, the professor's method of text selection seemed flawed, and I thought he was making some quite wild assumptions about the way words distrib-ute in the language. The way he used statistics was also questionable. However, what would the courts think? That was the issue.

I also noticed that Professor Willerby (not his real name), seemed to lack objectivity in writing his report. For instance, he stated that his task was to 'provide a report on the linguistic similarities between a set of texts (letters and emails) written by Mr. Bill Johnson and a different set of texts taken from X . . .' It seemed that the report writer had already made up his mind that there would be significant similarities and was just looking for evidence to support this view. Investigators into such issues should be completely impartial, and should state their terms in much more neutral language, for example, '. . . to provide a report on any possible linguistic similarity between x and y'. I also noted Willerby did not indicate that his report was being written for the benefit of any possible court or other trier of fact. Forensic linguists do not work for a client, even though they have to be commissioned by somebody – they work to assist the court.

In his preamble Willerby stated that

[the] field of forensic linguistics that focuses on such issues is known as Authorship Attribution. This field has a long history, known to the general public mainly through cases of contested authorship involving famous writers such as William Shakespeare. However, these methods have also been used in forensic studies such as the identification of the Unabomber based on a comparison between his personal notebook and his widely distributed manifesto.

There are several disturbing points about the above quotation if it is the view of an expert. The first is that forensic linguistics as a field is relatively new, and does not have a 'long history'. The term 'forensic linguistics' was first coined by Jan Svartvik in 1968. I once asked him how he had come up with the phrase and he said he used to watch a television series in the 1960s called *Quincy*. The word 'forensics' was always being mentioned and he thought it could be applied quite successfully to 'linguistics' as an adjective if the final 's' in forensics were dropped. It was in fact the title of the first ever paper on the subject.[1] However, the term was not in general use until about 1994 when the first academic journal with these words in its title was published. Moreover, authorship attribution is not exclusive to forensic linguistics. It is also common to literary poetics, where it has a much longer tradition. The authorship of Shakespeare is not a forensic matter: it is a populist dispute, with very little academic interest in that dispute (although there is some interest in the authorship issue), and, lastly, canonical literary authorship is an area of academic study which has no legal dimension whatsoever, and hence cannot be described as 'forensic linguistics'. Even Willerby's comments about the Unabomber are incorrect: he was initially identified on the basis of stylistic factors found in his letters to his brother and sister-in-law and not, as Willerby claimed, on the basis of his notebooks, which were only found after his arrest. I happen to have this information first hand from the distinguished FBI special agent who worked on the case, Jim Fitzgerald.

Talking about authorship attribution Willerby claims there are three procedures, which he cites as (i) informal analysis of linguistic idiosyncrasies, (ii) statistical analysis of the distribution of grammatical function words and (iii) the training of neural networks using artificial intelligence techniques.

Actually, Willerby appears to be confusing his terminology here. He begins by saying there are three main types of procedure. He then refers to 'general method', which he subsequently calls a 'procedure', then 'method' again, finally settling on 'technique'. This confusion of terminology leads me to believe that Willerby does not understand the difference between methods, procedures and techniques. He has not even discussed *approaches*.

It seems proper to begin with the idea of an *approach* to a problem. The most basic approach is a subjective assessment of idiosyncratic features, that is to say features which are or appear to be peculiar to a given author. This approach has its uses, but some consider it to be 'unscientific' because it cannot be easily quantified. The alternative approach is a quantitative one: any one of a number of quantitative techniques can be applied to any one of a number of linguistic features. The three basic areas of quantitative approach concern the measurement and statistical analysis of (i) the lexis (or vocabulary) of a text, (ii) grammatical (or function) words[2] and (iii) language modelling, for example by the use of compression algorithms, neural networks and so on. For each of these three approaches there are many possible methods of measurement and analysis.

Referring to his second 'method' Willerby says: 'The second general method involves statistical analysis of the distribution of "context free" words'. He then cites two authors, but although bibliographic references are given at the end, no actual page numbers are recorded. In a report, as with most academic work, it is essential to provide readers with the exact location of reference material. It is not sufficient to provide the name of a reference work, for the simple reason that others will not have all the information necessary to evaluate the report author's claims.

Willerby then claims, with reference to his second 'method', that 'this procedure has gained wide acceptance in the field', but I would dispute this. No single procedure has gained wide acceptance in the field. And, in any case, which field? If he means the field of forensic linguistics, this is simply not true: no linguist that I am aware of has presented authorship attribution to a court based on function word counts. If he means the field of computational linguistics, which has a strong interest in authorship questions, but is not in a position to make any input into forensic linguistics, that may be so. However, it should be noted that computational linguists usually work with very long texts, such as novels, long essays and other lengthy works. In forensic linguistics the reality is that most texts which are analysed are very short. It is not uncommon to undertake an inquiry with only three texts, each no longer than a few hundred words, and some even less than 50 words. For this reason forensic linguistic techniques tend to be somewhat different from those found in literary attribution work. In any case I was not aware of any computational linguist having given expert evidence in relation to a forensic authorship attribution claim.

In the context of expert reports it sometimes happens that authors will make a bold claim which cannot stand up to close cross-examination. Thus Willerby writes: 'Recently it has been argued that a complete syntactic analysis of both texts is a more direct method of achieving the same goal, although it is far more labour intensive and was not possible in the time allocated to the present analyses'. This seems to imply that Willerby has the necessary knowledge and software to undertake such a task and, most crucially, has experience at doing so. As far as I know, few analysts would ever attempt a 'complete' analysis on a 20,000 word document or set of documents, and in any case, carrying out syntactic analyses is a highly specialized task of which few linguists are capable.

Willerby also says: '[It] is generally accepted that the frequencies of a large number of these types of words form a kind of fingerprint for each writer'. However, although this may be 'generally accepted' it is not accepted by linguists who have had anything to do with authorship attribution. In fact it is contrary to much of what we understand about how language is acquired and used, and how it develops and atrophies throughout the human life cycle. As with his other claims Willerby gave no authorities for his claim that this notion is 'generally accepted'.

At one point in his analysis Willerby refers to a notorious authorship method which was rejected by the courts more than 10 years ago. It was known as the Cusum method and was developed by a vicar and a computer scientist. It was roundly attacked by linguists and psychologists alike. Under one of his headings: 'Function word analysis' Willerby claimed the Cusum technique had been rejected because 'the set of 2- and 3-letter words, plus words beginning with a vowel is not a natural linguistic category'. In fact, this is far from being the main reason the Cusum test was rejected. It was primarily rejected because it violates several basic scientific principles and is utterly ignorant of a number of elemental tenets of linguistics. I would have expected Willerby, given his position at a major educational institution, to know this. It also surprised me that an 'expert' would write a report on authorship attribution and then talk about a method that has long since been rejected by the entire forensic linguistic community.

Later, while still on the topic of function word analysis he says: 'In the early stages of authorship attribution research, it was thought that mean sentence length would be of value'. The irony here is that he is talking about work carried out by mathematicians a hundred years ago, beginning with Augustus de Morgan, TC Mendenhall and later Udney Yule. None of these mathematicians – distinguished though they were – had any connection with linguistics or even a serious interest in studying language. Therefore, to describe their work as 'the early phases of authorship attribution research' borders on the inventive. It was also puzzling to me as to why, once again, Willerby introduced a method, and then dismissed it by saying that it was not appropriate to the task of authorship attribution.

Still under the heading of 'function word analysis', Willerby then mentioned a measure known as type-token ratio. The type-token ratio is one of a number of ways linguists measure the richness of vocabulary in a specified length of text. The total length is the number of tokens, and the types are the total number of different words in the text being measured. However, type-token ratio is rarely a test undertaken of function words, mainly because it is used as a measure of a text's lexical richness. For this reason, I was surprised he mentioned it in the context of function (i.e. grammatical) words. More generally, it seems curious – once again – that he is describing a measure that has, as he admits, very little utility in authorship analyses.

Willerby says the Johnson texts and the X Material were supplied in hard copy format. Considering that the X Material was readily available on the internet, it seemed surprising that he then took printed text and scanned it using OCR techniques and then used various proofreading processes to ensure its accuracy. It seems somewhat strange for any analyst to imagine that he/she should transcribe an electronic document by first printing it, then scanning it and then proofreading it and in this way produce a version whose accuracy would be as good or better than the original electronic text. Willerby claims that 'each page was proofread by the OCR assistant'. He does not state whether this OCR assistant is a person or part of the software. OCR assistants exist in a number of software packages and generally 'help' with such matters as layout, text organization and so on. He says that a 'spell checker was used to correct errors if they did not appear in the original text'. I am not sure what this means. Does he mean that the spell checker used a standard spelling dictionary to remove errors, or does he mean that the spell checker was used to make sure that original errors were retained? I am not sure how a spell checker would do this: rather, this should have been carried out by Willerby himself.

The above points also apply to the known Bill Johnson texts. These were mostly email texts written by Mr Johnson at an earlier stage. If these were already electronic documents, why print them out and then scan and proofread them? Some earlier OCR (which stands for Optical Character Recognition) scanning packages were notorious for being processor intensive and for producing multiple errors, especially from documents such as emails. Incidentally, the word 'error' has to be used advisedly here. An error in this context does not mean a grammatical, orthographic, spelling or punctuation error. Rather, it refers to whether the scanning process produces text which is *different* from the source text. If the scanner faithfully re-produces an item of text which is itself an error, then – in the forensic context this is not an error. It is correct. On the other hand, if the scanner 'corrects' an error, through – for example – its inherent spell-checking device – then this is an error, even though what is produced is grammatically, orthographically, and in other ways correct. The usual purpose of a spell checker in OCR scanning software, is to correct the spelling mistakes which the software finds: however, in the forensic context it is important *not* to 'correct' anything, since a forensic text must always be presented *as is*.

I very much doubt that anyone is able to proofread 20,000 words to such a high standard that it would be, in the context of scanning, error-free, especially if working under time constraints (which Willerby hints at elsewhere in his report). Even the most careful author will produce errors of various kinds, and if the OCR scanning process did not identify these, or misrepresented them in some way, then Willerby's version of the X Material was quite possibly not an accurate representation of the original source material. The same may apply to Mr Johnson's own texts. Willerby did not provide copies of the texts he used to compile his report. Johnson requested sight of the emails he wrote which were used as the texts to be tested against – which are termed 'exemplar texts', but Willerby refused this request. This is a most unusual procedure, given that it means that at this time the test documents in this case cannot be verified either as to provenance or accuracy.

Willerby's next heading was 'Selection of samples'. As far as I could tell the only methods he had so far described also happened to be ones he rejected. He had still not stated what methods he intended to use to carry out his 'attribution'. Moreover, in forensic work, the questioned texts are never described as *samples*. They are the obligatory set of texts, since the whole object of the exercise is to discover the identity of their author or, more scientifically, to discover what basis one would have for rejecting or failing to reject one or other candidate author.

But the most serious linguistic weakness in Willerby's report was yet to come. It was to do with the text types of the exemplar texts. Willerby said that these were all examples of 'expository prose'. Expository prose is simply a technical term for writing which is intended to explain something – usually technical. Some of Willerby's non-suspect exemplars do indeed fall into the category of 'expository prose': for example he includes in his corpus of non-suspect exemplar texts an undergraduate essay and a portion of a doctoral thesis in linguistics (his own perhaps?). However, we may question whether Bill Johnson's emails – even if on fairly formal topics – would entirely qualify as 'expository prose', since texts written in asynchronous electronic media[3] are usually much less structured than more formal prose, and are likely to be informal in addressivity and tone. Moreover, we may even question whether one of the texts included in Willerby's corpus, a lecture given to undergraduates which he himself wrote, qualifies as prose in the traditional sense of the word, since it was written to be spoken or read aloud to a group, rather than written to be read by individual readers. I wondered why he had chosen 'expository prose' as his criterion of classification. The X Material was definitely not expository prose. If anything, it was mild political satire.

I was also somewhat surprised he had used his own work in an author-ship investigation. In nearly 15 years of forensic linguistic work I had never heard of anyone doing this. In the context of forensic work, this is completely unprofessional, and seems to demonstrate inexperience in the forensic field. A comparable example would be the election researcher who, in order to increment the apparent support among a population of sample voters for a particular political party, records his/her own voting intentions as part of the election poll he/she is researching. We would certainly consider that such a procedure on the part of that researcher would have a prejudicial effect on the poll results. I doubt very much whether any academic researcher would ever include his/her own work in a corpus to be studied, unless very particular circumstances applied, which I do not believe to be the case here.

So, what we are seeing here is that there is a complete mix of text and genre types, leading to a somewhat mixed register, which I will describe in more detail below. Before I go on to talk about register, however, it is worth noting the diversity of text types, as well as the genre mix, in Willerby's corpus of sample texts. As regards text type, we have lectures, emails, an essay and a thesis. In most authorship attribution analyses I have carried out or studied it is usual to ensure homogeneity of text type among exem-plar texts, unless there are practical reasons for not doing so, for example if the questioned text is of a particularly rare type. This does certainly not apply in the present instance. However, I can understand that Willerby used Mr Johnson's emails simply because he had no other exemplar texts of Mr Johnson's writings available – but in that case he should have con-fined himself to emails or, at worst, just used emails and web journal texts for comparison purposes. The genre mix is also worth noting: we have academic texts combined with texts relating to committee administration, and these in turn are being compared with anonymous items critical to the management of a flying club. This can scarcely be described as an homogenous corpus with regard to genre. Finally, Willerby did not appear to take on board the notion that he was dealing, not just with texts whose authorship was unknown, but with anonymous or concealed authorship. Willerby does not appear to consider the possibility that anonymous authors may attempt to disguise their work, just as anonymous phone callers will try to disguise their voice. There is no doubt that authorial attempts at disguise can affect the outcome of any testing procedure.

To come back to *register*, then, it is a further term that we need to discuss to understand where Willerby was going wrong. The concept of register concerns such questions as how a text is produced, to whom it is addressed, whether it is formal in its structure and content and so on. Register is considered to consist of three sub-areas:

1. *Mode* refers to language channel and concerns such issues as whether a text was produced by means of writing, speaking or dictating; whether it was produced in one form but delivered in another (e.g. news bulletins written to be spoken, lectures etc); whether a visual or interactive module was delivered concurrently with the language (e.g. photographs, cartoons in a newspaper, or charts and tables in an academic journal). Hence, when comparing texts for authorship, or any other linguistic analysis, it is important to have uniformity of *language mode*. There has been a considerable amount of research on asynchronous electronic media, such as emails and cell phone texts, in recent years, and these are considered to have many features in common with spoken language. As a result, I do not believe we can safely say that a useful comparison can be made between emails and dissertations, or emails and web journal text, for example. The fact that one of the exemplar texts is a lecture which was written to be spoken aloud to an audience, while another is an email addressed to a colleague, while yet another is an undergraduate essay, shows that Willerby does not appear to have taken register factors seriously which, given his claimed linguistic background, is somewhat surprising. He appears to be asserting that all of his sample texts are 'expository prose' and that this is sufficiently narrow a classification to ensure some kind of corpus homogeneity. I think any linguist would contest this point.

2. *Tenor* is a sub-area of register which is concerned with the relationship between the text producer and the recipient, that is, writer-reader,

speaker-hearer, lecturer-audience and so on. In the previous section I described how the mix of language modalities would mitigate against useful comparisons being possible between the exemplar texts and the X Material, and I maintain that the same point applies to issues of linguistic *tenor*. Thus, a student writing an essay addresses that essay to his/her professor for grading. The writer of an email may or may not know his/her addressee, but the writer–reader relationship in this instance is not necessarily going to be directly comparable to the student-professor relationship which is itself an apparent inverse of the professor–student audience relationship applicable to the lecture environment (given that Willerby includes a lecture in his exemplar corpus). For this reason, in authorship attribution analysis it is usual to choose exemplars which match the questioned texts with regard to *tenor* issues.

3. *Field* is a critical register issue. It concerns, broadly, the topic area of a text or set of texts and, what the language of the text is designed to do (in the performative sense). The field properties of the exemplar texts chosen by Willerby are as varied as are their mode and tenor properties. For example, we have advanced academic prose about linguistics (in the graduate thesis), emails about committees and administration, a lecture on linguistics and an undergraduate essay on an unspecified topic. The suspect candidate's exemplar texts consist of emails to his flying club about aviation and club matters. This is a fairly close match with the questioned texts, the X Material, but no match at all with the non-suspect exemplar texts mentioned above: however, the match only extends to *field* not to text type, and as previously commented on, the variety of text type is likely to mitigate against a useful authorship attribution comparison being possible. By constructing his corpus in this way, Willerby has biased his test procedure in favour of choosing Johnson as the most likely author.

4. *Other sociolinguistic issues:* We do not know the respective ages and gender/s of most of the candidate authors, nor their level of education. More critically, no mention is made in Willerby's report of any attempt to match sociolinguistic criteria. It is the usual practice, in authorship analysis, where a likely pool of candidates is not available alongside a suspect candidate (e.g. other personnel at a company or organization where the chief suspect candidate is also employed), to then attempt to match the candidate pool to the suspect, just as one would do in an identification parade. For example, we could not easily imagine an identification parade with

a tall, bald man of middle age, a short, fat hairy, young one, a young woman, an elderly person of either gender and so on. Further, in an ideal investigation we would probably want to ensure that our candidates came from the same geographical area, that they followed fairly similar occupations at similar levels, and that all of the texts were written within a fairly narrow timespan. Willerby makes no mention of any of these points.

In his report Willerby appears to accept implicitly that the authorship of the X texts is single in character. He does exclude 'letters to the editor' and other clearly non-candidate aspects of the texts, but he fails to mention the possibility that there might be more than one author of the X texts. However, we should bear in mind that it is not uncommon for publications of all types to attribute authorship to one individual, yet have several editors or contributors who are not specifically named. Moreover, it is also not unusual, in journals of all kinds, for two or more authors to collaborate in the writing of one text and for texts to be edited for a particular house style. Therefore, a lay reader of Willerby's report might think that it is safe to assume that the authorship of the text is single, and this could act on reader sensibilities in a prejudicial way since the possibility of any multiple-author configuration has not been considered.

In summary, Willerby's work did not constitute a professional report of a standard expected of courts as an aid to triers of fact. There were several reasons for this:

- His text selection is flawed because he mixes his own work with that of others. He pays no regard to questions of genre, text type, mode, field or tenor. He disregards sociological issues such as age, gender and level of education. He altogether avoids questions of dual authorship and author disguise.
- He did not seem to be aware of the fact that function words are not wholly context free, and he seems to consider both mean sentence length and type-token ratio are related to questions of function word analysis. In addition, his method of text preparation was suspect. Why did he decide to scan in electronic texts? How accurate was the product?
- No theoretical input is given to support his claims: we do not know why he believes authors can have a linguistic fingerprint when, in fact, there are strong reasons to believe the opposite: for example, the realization that language is a socially acquired property not an

inherited one, that it is subject to influence and change, and that it is susceptible to macro-socially homogenizing influences such as education and the media.

In my professional view, Willerby's understanding of the topic and selection of his corpus rendered the entire report worthless. I will, nevertheless demonstrate, in the following sections two further areas of gross error, namely that his method of linguistic analysis is flawed, as is his method of statistical reporting. In order to explain my position I will now talk about the two main types of word we find in language. These are *lexical words* and *function words*. Lexical words are assumed to hold meaning, and this class includes nouns, adjectives, verbs and certain adverbs. Function words, on the other hand, do not contain independent meaning, but, effectively, carry the grammar of the language, and include such categories as prepositions, determiners and function adverbs. This is the traditional division of words into types or levels of semantic structure, as originally advanced by Henry Sweet as 'sense-units' (i.e. lexical words) and 'form-words' (i.e. function words), (Sweet, 1891: 22).

In his section 'Selection of samples' it is somewhat difficult to follow Willerby's procedure. Apparently he took the 50 most frequent words for each text set, and from these retained only those which were 'context-free'. He says he discarded 'context-dependent' words such as 'taxi-way'. I am not clear here whether he means that he discarded all lexical words, or only those lexical words which he deemed to be context-dependent. What was his basis for, or definition of context dependence? In any case, the whole issue of context-dependence in terms of function words needs to be challenged. We may think that a function word would not depend on context for its distribution, but this is not true of all of them. Some function words show the same distribution whatever the genre or text type, and hence are context free in terms of distribution. On the other hand, some have a different distribution, dependent on text type or genre, and so are not context-free.

If, then, the test corpus consists of different text types, it follows that the test procedure will skew the results of those frequency words and not paint an accurate picture when comparing the questioned with the known text. Below, I illustrate this point by giving some examples of function word frequencies for different text types based on some simple word-count software. In the first instance I looked for word frequencies in a medium similar to the questioned texts, namely newspaper articles. I then compared word frequencies in this medium with that of emails – a text type

Table 14.1. Distribution of 'the' and 'a/an' in a small corpus of news articles and email texts

Word	News	Email
the	0.074	0.044
a/an	0.027	0.026

Table 14.2. Distribution of selected singular/dual pronouns in a small corpus of news articles and email texts

Word	News	Email
I	0.00	0.04
you	0.00	0.02
he/she	0.01	0.01

used in Willerby's corpus. I decided to use just the most common function words, namely the definite and indefinite determiners. The results were as shown in Table 14.1. As can be seen from Table 14.1, although the 'a/an' distribution is similar across the two text types, distribution of 'the' across the two text types is significantly different. In fact there are sound linguistic reasons for this, since newspaper articles are most often about something other than first and second grammatical persons (i.e. 'I', 'you' etc), whereas emails are most often either about 'you' and 'I' or necessarily include 'you' and 'I' in order to carry out a conversation about something else. This is clearly demonstrated when we come to measure the same test corpus for selected personal pronouns (singular/dual) as seen in Table 14.2.

From Table 14.2 we see that the selected first and second personal pronouns are virtually non-existent in news articles, but of relatively high frequency in email texts. Hence, results from Tables 14.1 and 14.2 appear to indicate that if comparing texts of different types then we should *not* rely on frequency counts of some common function words for authorship purposes: the text type and genre influences are likely to skew the result. For example, if we took emails and news articles for the same writer, there is no reason to believe that we would not find that exemplars of each text type would follow the above pattern.

This is why we need to treat terms such as 'context-free' and 'context-dependent' with some caution. While function words may be context-free in theory, or less context-dependent than lexical words, it does not seem that the concept of 'context-dependence' is a useful one when we are undertaking such a precise task as authorship attribution.

Authorship attribution is a serious task, especially where people's reputations, liberty and even, on occasion, lives, are at stake and definitions which may be useful in academic discussions, are not necessarily useful when applied to precise and important tasks such as authorship attribution. Following presentation of my analysis to the court, the flying club withdrew their allegations against Mr Johnson and paid him substantial damages for the distress they had caused him. Nobody knows quite what the management of the club were thinking when they launched this action against one of their most loyal members. At one point Mr Johnson observed officials from the club photographing his young grandchildren playing in the garden from a parked car, which is equally inexplicable behaviour.[4]

As to Professor Willerby I have not heard of any further ventures of his into forensic linguistics, and while I wish him a long and successful career in his chosen field, I trust that that will remain the case until such time as he acquires the appropriate knowledge and experience to deal with issues which are, at the present time, outside of his customary domain.

Notes

1. Svartvik, Jan (1968). *The Evans Statements: A Case for Forensic Linguistics*. Gothenburg: Acta Universitatis Gothoburgensis.
2. Linguists consider that the lexicon (vocabulary) is divided into two main categories: lexical words and function words. A lexical word is a content word, such as 'happy', 'table', 'love' and so on. A function word helps to convey the grammar and has no intrinsic meaning. Thus, 'the' is a function word, as is 'of', 'any', 'into' and so on.
3. Asynchronous electronic media are messages to which the reply is delayed (hence 'asynchronous'). This would refer to emails, phone text messages, ICQ and chatroom messages and so on.
4. I am not suggesting for a moment that Prof. Willerby had anything to do with this.

Reference

Sweet, H. (1891). *A New English Grammar*. Part II, Syntax. Oxford: Clarendon Press (Reference here is to the 1968 impression).

15

ON DEATH ROW

On the afternoon of Wednesday 18 May 1994, in the state of South Carolina, Joseph and Barbara Lafayette died of gunshot wounds at their home at Adams Run near the city of Charleston. On the following day a young man travelling through the state was arrested and later tried and found guilty of the crime. He is currently on death row at Lieber Correctional Institute at Ridgeville, SC. His South Carolina Department of Corrections number is 5041. His name is James Earl Reed and at the time of his arrest he had not long been released from the federal penitentiary in Kentucky. He was on his way back home to North Carolina when he was arrested not far from Charleston. As it happened, he had been acquainted with the Lafayettes before going to prison. The killing had been viewed by the prosecution as a grudge murder because James had once dated their daughter. The young couple had fallen out and James had allegedly driven a vehicle at the daughter's new boyfriend in anger. This was why he had been serving a sentence in Kentucky. It was alleged that he had come back to South Carolina to seek revenge against the girl. Unable to find her he had shot the girl's parents in anger. After his conviction, James Earl Reed sat on death row for nearly 12 years, trying to get people to listen to his side of the case. He claimed that the statement written out by the detectives was not what he had said. Finally, he made contact with a private investigator by the name of Philip Upton. Upton listened to Reed's story and then sent me a copy of the statement and examples of Reed's written language. The wheels of justice grind slowly all over the world, and this is particularly true of people on death row. James Earl Reed has learned to be patient, but he still maintains his innocence.

The statement attributed to Reed is about 1,500 words long. I am giving this statement in full at the end of this chapter because it will be helpful in understanding the facts of this case.

It is in the handwriting of Detective D. R. Hale of the Charleston County Sheriff's Office, Charleston, South Carolina, and is dated 19 May 1994. The statement describes how Mr Reed left the federal penitentiary at Manchester, Kentucky in April 1994, how he arrived at the city of Greenville, purchased a weapon and some ammunition and how he then travelled to Charleston, South Carolina, arriving on 17 May, the day before the shooting at Adams Run. The statement describes how Reed contacted Mrs Lafayette on the evening of 17 May, of how he passed the night in the open air near a shopping mall and of how he went to the Lafayette house on 18 May, met with the Lafayettes and shot them, then departed the scene in their car and drove to a nearby dirt track called Scott White Road where, according to the statement, he ditched their vehicle and got rid of the gun and casings. The statement concludes with how Reed was arrested the following morning. Along with the statement there is also a document labelled 'Incident Report', and this is also in Detective Hale's handwriting. These notes cover the night of 18 May 1994, and describe how Hale had been informed by radio that a shooting had taken place at Adams Run, Charleston, and that he was then requested to attend the local university medical hospital. The notes also cover the events of the following day when the defendant, James Earl Reed, was interviewed by Detectives Hale and Coaxum. A third page of notes deals with some administrative matters relating to the case several days later. Here is an excerpt from the detective's notes for 19 May 1994:

5-19-94

0950: Interview suspect – Verbally mirandize – have suspect (James Reed) sign written Miranda waiver. Det. S. Coaxum is present.

I/O left room and allowed Det. Coaxum to speak to suspect

1100 Det. Coaxum advises I/O that suspect had admitted to shooting the two victims and would show deputies where the gun had been thrown into the woods

1130 Leave headquarters with suspect

1200 Arrive on Hwy. 162 near Towles Road – search in woods for gun.

Landmarks – White fence, dark fence, white rocks near drive, stump across highway – on 162 east of Towles Road.

Assisting in search – Det. Fields, Tittle, Lt Smoak, Dep McMicking, Deputy Presnell, Det. Coaxum

Failed to locate gun in the woods

Proceed to Scott White Road – to location where suspect ditched vehicle dirt lane off Scott White Road that connects with Towles Road

Proceed to Scott White Road at sharp curve – gravel piles – Reed stated that he threw casings out the window at the curve.

Did not locate casings.

According to Detective Hale's notes, he and Detective Coaxum began interviewing Mr Reed at 9.50 a.m. in the morning when the suspect was cautioned[1] (or 'mirandized' as the process is referred to in the United States of America). At some unspecified point in the interview, Hale left the interview room and when he returned the other detective, Coaxum, informed him that the suspect had admitted to shooting the victims and would show officers where the weapon had been discarded. One of the first questions of importance in a linguistic investigation is the relationship between the documents exhibited and the events they purport to describe. Part of the process of discovering this relationship is to do with the timeframe. In the present instance I was interested in *when* the incident notes had come to be written. There was no easy way to tell. The notes contain an entry on 23 May, 4 days after the interview with the suspect, and so may have been written even later than that. Chronology is important because if the notes were written out several days after the events they purport to describe, then how can we be sure the writer was accurate in his recall of those events? I noted that the report started out using the past tense, then switched to the historical present, and then reverted again to the past tense. You can see this in the excerpt of the notes given above. This combination of tenses led me to believe that the incident notes could be a kind of summary narrative, suggesting that they had only been completed several days after the statement had been taken. In any event, although we cannot be sure exactly when the incident notes were compiled, they could have been written at any time up until 15 June 1994, when they were stamped by the police department as having been 'received'. Although the report is nominally in the name of the detective completing it, Detective Hale, I wondered whether Hale may have consulted Coaxum when completing them. Later I will show the relationship between these notes and the alleged statement.

In the opening paragraph of Page 2, under the heading '0950', the report states 'I/O [Det Hale] left room and allowed Det. Coaxum to speak to suspect'. At '11:00' the report states that 'Det Coaxum advises I/O [Det Hale] that suspect had admitted to shooting the two victims'.

Since these are Hale's own notes, it seems reasonable to ask why he refers to himself in the third person in his own report, that is, as 'I/O' – which means 'investigating officer'. I suggest that this phrase may have come from another written source, and that that source was probably Coaxum's notes, for example, 'I/O left room', 'I advised I/O that . . .' and so on. If this is true, then it is even possible that Detective Coaxum's notes are not contemporaneous. The reason I say this is that if Coaxum had written his notes contemporaneously he is much more likely to have written 'I/O leaving room' or 'I/O leaves room'. I also suggest that it is singular that there is no record of the actual time that Detective Hale left the room nor of the time he returned to it. We can perhaps assume that he returned at 11 a.m., because that is when Detective Coaxum informs him of Mr Reed's alleged admission. Since this is important news he is not likely to have waited to tell Hale, and Hale is not likely to have been in the room when Mr Reed made this admission, since there would not have been any need to tell Hale of the admission had he been present.

The statement time record gives a slightly different chronology. It states that the morning interview session began at 9.50 a.m. and ended at 10.30 a.m., while the report states that Detective Hale was not informed of Mr Reed's admission until 11.00 a.m. Since the reason the session was ended is given as the need to search for the weapon, then it is an important question as to when the interview actually ended. We note from Hale's incident notes that the statement itself was not actually obtained until the evening.

There were a number of common features between the statement and the incident notes which gave me cause for concern. Hale's report states how the detectives left the office at 11.30 a.m. to search for the weapon which they claim Mr Reed offered to assist them to do. In the statement we read that Mr Reed left the Lafayette residence in the victims' car, drove to Highway 162, and then turned off that road onto Scott White Road in order to dispose of the car. He then apparently runs into the woods, discards the weapon and emerges back onto Highway 162, apparently sees a stump and a dark and a white fence, and then goes back to Highway 17, to the Circle K, the fuel and food convenience chain.

According to the report, Detective Hale begins the search for the weapon at the woods where the landmarks – the stump, the dark and the white fence – are located. It is interesting that Detective Hale's account in his notes follows the exact *reverse* sequence of that described in the statement. This is shown in more detail in the Table 15.1. The

Table 15.1. Table showing that the events in Detective Hale's incident report are in the exact reverse sequence of those given in the alleged statement of J. E. Reed

1	white fence	7	. . . first left turn on Scott White Road . . . threw [casings] out of the window
2	dark fence	6	. . . looking for a place to ditch the car . . .
3	White ~~gravel~~ rocks near drive		
4	stump across highway	5	. . . threw the gun away in the woods
	. . .	4	. . . ran out to the roadway and saw a tree stump
5	Failed to locate gun in the woods	3	On the other side of the road was a driveway with large white rocks
6	Proceed to Scott White Road – to location where suspect ditched vehicle . . .	2	. . . nearby was a dark wooden fence.
		1	A little further down was a white wooden fence.
7	Proceed to Scott White Road at sharp curve – gravel piles – Reed stated that he threw casings out the window at the curve . . .		

landmarks Detective Hale refers to in his report are given as follows:

'. . . white fence, dark fence, white rocks near drive . . . stump across highway'.

In James Earl Reed's statement the landmarks are given as follows:

'. . . tree stump, drive with large white rocks, dark fence, white fence'.

As we can see from the above these two versions are in reverse order of each other.

As a result, it becomes clear that either the statement is dependent on the report or the report is dependent on the statement, since it seems beyond coincidence that there should be an exact reverse match of so many items. The questions attached to this finding are (i) why and (ii) how?

The 'why' concerns the reasons and the 'how' concerns the method of carrying out the match. Hale was in charge of his own notes and he was in charge of the production of the statement. Either he took the notes at the investigation site at the time of the events and then simply reversed the order when he came to write out the statement, or he prepared his own notes using the statement. Given that it is likely the investigative report was written only several days after the arrest and incarceration of Mr Reed, it is more likely that he used the statement to compile his report. If this is true then this means his own notes were incomplete because he was now relying on the statement for the 'correct' version of events. But why? Surely this level of accuracy was not necessary? It would have been sufficient in his report to say something like 'went to landmarks mentioned by suspect in wooded area adjacent to Highway 162'. This level of precision, also evident elsewhere in the statement, is more typical of *police register* (see definition of 'police register' below) than it is of ordinary everyday language. In my view this level of cross-matching between the statement and Hale's investigative report forces us to doubt either the report or the statement or both. The fact that the order of events and landmarks is reversed, gives a strong indication, in my view, that Detective Hale was attempting to disguise the fact that he was copying from one document to produce the other. It is the kind of technique often used by students when plagiarizing from the internet or other sources in order to mask the fact that they are copying. It would be for a court to determine these facts, and to ascertain what it was that motivated Detective Hale to carry out such an extraordinary procedure when compiling the case documents. An Esda examination of the original documents may assist the process and can be carried out by any well equipped forensic laboratory. Such an examination should include any other notes held by Detective Hale and all of the notes held by Detective Coaxum, as well as any custody record at the police headquarters kept by other staff.

As one possible explanation for the reverse matching of events I considered the possibility that Hale and Coaxum wished to begin their search where the explanation in the statement ended, namely, the point at which the suspect allegedly discarded the weapon. It could be argued that the detectives then worked backwards from that point. This is plausible to a degree (though the exact reverse match of the events leading up to the discarding of the weapon is not so credible), but it still does not explain why the landmarks would be given in reverse order. In any case, the statement was not taken down until the evening. So, unless we can obtain more detailed contemporaneous notes of the detectives' visit to the investigation site we are unlikely to know exactly how the reverse match, described above, came about. We can sum up the outstanding questions surrounding the two documents as follows: How long after the incidents was the report written? How much does the report rely on Detective Hale's memory? How much does it rely on the memory of Detective Coaxum? How much does it rely on the words of the suspect's statement?

Above I referred to 'police register'. In police statements it is sometimes found that police officers will report the language of a suspect in what is known as 'police speak' or police register, that is to say language which is institutional or official in character, as opposed to the normal everyday language we would associate with most speakers. Because this often leads to the content of statements being disputed, many police departments throughout the United States now either tape-record suspect interviews or ask suspects and witnesses to complete statements in their own hand-writing. Because of the nature of police work, it is noticeable that police register has a number of characteristics which set it apart from ordinary everyday language. The main requirement of police language is that it needs to be efficient and compact. This leads to set phrases, dense word-ing in an impersonal, official style with precise renditions of time, place and sequence and precise descriptions of objects. In the statement we have a number of examples of such phenomena as shown in Table 15.2.

The statement (see copy at the end of this chapter) gives an apparently coherent narrative of the alleged events surrounding the shooting of Mr and Mrs Lafayette. However, the language of the statement indicates that at least some of its content is unlikely to have originated with an ordinary speaker, but in a number of instances the language has a strong resemblance to police register. It is disturbing that there are so many examples of attempts at technical, factual or linguistic precision. In the next section I will give examples of Mr Reed's own written language. It will be seen that Mr Reed is far from linguistically competent.

At trial it was stated by Detective Hale that he wrote the statement based on Mr Reed's verbal account. This is entirely normal procedure but it does beg the question as to how much of the content may be Mr Reed's and how much may be that of the detectives. We may rea-sonably ask ourselves: 'What does *based on* mean?' The presence of a number of police register examples above indicates that there is a pos-sibility that a substantial amount of the phrasing originated with the detectives, rather than with Mr Reed.

Because I do not have any samples of Mr Reed's speech I will therefore be using his written language as an indication of how he expresses him-self. In doing so it is necessary to bear in mind the differences between the language of the statement and Mr Reed's letters:

i.   There is an 11 year gap between the two, indicating the possibility of extensive changes in Mr Reed's language, especially given the fact that he has been incarcerated for a long period since the state-ment was given.

ii. Police statements and letters are completely different text types. The first is an official communication usually prepared for the bene-fit of the court, while the second is a personal communication.

iii. The topics contained within the letters are of a different nature than those found within the statement. Whereas the statement deals with the events surrounding the deaths of Mr and Mrs Lafayette, the letters deal mainly with Mr Reed's requests to Mr Upton regard-ing his determination to prove his innocence.

Table 15.2. Examples of the language of the statement

Example	Comment
a silvery-colored, somewhat rusty 9 mm semi-automatic pistol	A long nominal phrase including a compound adjective (silvery-colored), a qualifier ('somewhat'), a qualitative assessment adjective ('rusty'), a technical description of bore ('9 mm'), a further compound adjective, ('semi-automatic'), a noun ('pistol').
	Unlikely to be used by most ordinary speakers in this way. Probably several phrases in the original. It is also likely to be a technical description by someone professionally familiar with firearms, that is, a police officer. Note especially '9 mm' and 'pistol'.
I ended up in Charleston at about 6.30 p.m. on May 17th, 1994	Speaker is more likely to have said 'the day before yesterday in the evening' or something similar.
I called Barbara from the Circle K store at Highway 17 across from the Mazda dealer. Also a BP Gas Mart is next door.	An ordinary speaker is unlikely to have given such a detailed geographical description in one phrase, especially if he was not familiar with the area.
I left my nylon carry bag	The phrase is unlikely to have been spoken like this, especially the word 'nylon'.
personal items	Sounds like official language, used by police departments, hospitals and so on.
Barbara and Joseph pulled up in their **small two-door red car**.	Precise nominal phrase containing a series of adjectives and adjectival phrases. Sounds like an official description. Given the circumstances would the suspect, or any ordinary speaker, have remembered that the car had *two* doors? The word order (position of 'red') is also unusual.
the slide on the gun was locked back	Sounds like someone who knows about firearms
I picked the shell casings up off the floor . . . I put the cases in my **right front pants pocket**.	Description is too precise and detailed for a single phrase.
I drove past **four black males**	Sounds very precise as to number. Also 'males' sounds like a police description.
I got the **9 mm** casings out of my **right front pocket**	We already know they are '9 mm'. It is unnecessary information at this point. It seems like an effort to tie the suspect to the casings. Also, 'right front pocket' is unnecessary for the same reason'. In this context 'pocket' would have been sufficient.
I *then* ran out to the roadway **and saw a tree stump. On the other side of the road was a driveway with large white rocks, and nearby was a dark wooden fence. A little further down was a white wooden fence.**	A very detailed description of a scene and one unlikely to have been remembered in this amount of detail by an ordinary speaker. Note also the position of *then*, which is often cited by linguists as a sign of police register.

Balanced against the above considerations, all of which would tend to cause some differentiation between the two text types, the main aspect of Mr Reed's language I will be looking at concerns his level of language ability, with his IQ reported by psychologists at the time of his trial to be 77, which is borderline functional. Mr Reed's written language indicates a low level of language ability. He does not always appear to know the difference between how to use an adjective and a noun, and other categories of speech; many of his sentences run into each other and there is almost no punctuation. An example is given below:

THE TRUTH

A INNOCENCE MAN A <u>INNOCENCE</u> LADY TELL THEIR POLICE DETECTIVE INVESTIGATOR THE TRUTH THAT THEY ARE INNOCENCE YET THAT INNOCENCE MAN THAT INNOCENCE LADY NOW GO TO JAIL WERE THEY AWAIT A PUBLIC DEFENDER WHO FROM THE VARIOUS STEREOTYPES PUT UPON VARIOUS CRIMES MEET YOU THINKING YOU ARE GUILTY YET I HAVE TO <u>LISTEN WERE</u> THE INNOCENCE MAN OR LADY DONT KNOW ANY BETTER THEY TRUST THE PUBLIC DEFENDER WHILE AWAITING TRIAL THAN COME TRIAL THE PUBLIC DEFENDER PUT ON A SHOW IN COURT DOING HIS OR HER JOB WERE THE INNOCENCE MAN OR LADY DONT KNOW ANYTHING ESLE YET THEIR LAWYER MAKE THEM LOOK AND SOUND GUILTY THAN THAT INNOCENCE MAN OR LADY NOW GO TO PRISON NOW GO TO DEATH ROW

WAKE UP

From the above excerpt we see that Mr Reed's written language is very striking. I have underlined some of the words I will be referring to. The function of 'listen', line 6, is uncertain. Does he mean 'you have to listen', or does he mean 'I have to state (so that you listen)'? The meaning of 'were' is uncertain. Is it a misspelling for 'where', for example? Note also the usage of 'innocence' as an adjective. In a number of cases we cannot be sure where one sentence ends and another begins, for example: 'Yet I have to listen were the innocence man or lady dont know any better they trust the public defender while awaiting trial'. Only five clausal conjunctions are used ('yet' × 3, 'than' × 2) further adding to difficulty of interpretation. The style of the language is extremely repetitive, with 'innocence' used no less than eight times in the 123-word excerpt shown here. Measurement of many texts over the years leads me to believe that a word used more than twice in the space of 100 words would be perceived by most readers as repetitive. The lexical density of the text is low for such a short text: it is only 51 per cent, but for an excerpt of this length I would expect a density of at least 60 per cent for text which originated as written language. A similar excerpt from the statement gives a lexical density of 57 per cent which, I suggest, is higher than one would expect from language which originated as speech, thus indicating – in my view – that it owes as much to writing as it does to speech.

As we can see from the above example, Mr Reed's use of language is both obsessive and repetitive. It is also ambiguous. Grammatically it lacks even the basics of successful communication and leaves a heavy burden of interpretation on the reader. Hence, Reed cannot be described as an articulate user of the language, which may be reflective of the remarks of the psychologist regarding his general level of intelligence. In contrast to the writings of the letters, the language of the statement reflects an articulate user of the language, someone who is able to express himself more than adequately by, for example, presenting a coherent narrative of some complexity and length. Some of this discrepancy may be due to the length of Mr Reed's incarceration, and some may be due to the detective's skill as an interpreter of what Mr Reed may have told him. However, I still believe there is a discrepancy because Hale was in all probability obliged to work out what happened from short answers to questions, most often probably no more than a few words in length.

According to Hale the statement commenced being taken at 16:30 hrs and was completed at 19:50 hrs. Thus, a 1500-word statement takes some 200 minutes to write out, which is an average of 7 words per minute. Most people experienced at taking down defendant and witness statements average approximately 25 words per minute. I suggest the reportedly slow pace of the statement in this case adds weight to the idea that the language of the statement most probably originated as a question and answer session. Mindful of the identical reverse sequence of a section of the investigative report and the part of the statement that deals with the drive from the Lafayette's house to the point where the weapon was allegedly discarded, it seems plausible that Detective Hale used his notes to compile that section of the statement that deals with the events leading up to the alleged discarding of the weapon.

I believe that many of the things attributed to Mr Reed were not said by him. It does not seem conceivable, for example, that he described the weapon as a 'silvery-colored, somewhat rusty 9 mm semi-automatic pistol'. The phrase is simply too dense and too technical for someone of such poor abilities as Mr Reed to utter – see also 'the slide on the gun was locked back'. Other phrases are simply too detailed, or provide unnecessary information, for example '*nylon* carry bag'. Others, like 'personal items' are much more likely to be indicative of official language. The detail about the car, a 'small two-door red car' is not only unlikely to have been uttered by Mr Reed, it also condenses too much observation into so short a stretch of language. The word 'nonchalant' to describe Joseph Lafayette is not a word I would associate with Mr Reed's vocabulary ability. I find the detail about allegedly having placed the shell casings in his 'right front pants pocket' incredible. Again, it is not only very precise it is also extremely dense. It contains the kind of detail most people would not think to remark on or even remember. However, the detail that seems most beyond belief is the description of the landmarks. Why would Mr Reed remember in such detail the landmarks around the area where he was supposed to have thrown the gun? It directly contradicts the idea, previously expressed, that he did not hide the gun, but threw it behind him – suggesting that he did not care where the gun was. This part of the statement, 'I *then* ran out to the roadway and saw a tree stump. On the other side of the road was a driveway with large white rocks, and nearby was a dark wooden fence. A little further down was a white wooden fence' is at a level of observation that only someone accustomed to noting such details would make, rather than an ordinary individual of significantly low intelligence. Note also the position of the word *then* in 'I *then* ran out'. It is in a postposed position and replaces the more usual 'Then I ran out'. This is typical of police register, the language of official police communications and has been cited by many linguists in this regard (see Olsson 2004[2]).

The statement also appears to contain at least one factual inaccuracy. It quotes Mrs Lafayette as asking Mr Reed why he had given up trucking. Mr Reed states that he had never followed the occupation of a trucker, and according to his legal advisers there is no evidence of his having followed this occupation. I also find it less than credible that someone who is not a native of South Carolina, and who could not have been very familiar with the area would give such detailed descriptions of so many locations, including names of places, roads, stores and other facilities including the highway system in the state. Many of these descriptions reveal a familiarity with the geography of the area which could simply not have been acquired in the short time that Mr Reed had been in the state. This degree of precision about location and place names is also a feature of police register, given that police officers are required by their profession to be observant about such matters. Mr Reed's limited intellectual and linguistic abilities make it even less likely that he was able to recall places, names and routes with the degree of precision shown in the statement.

For the reasons stated above, in addition to the observations made earlier about the provenance of the investigative report with regard to the somewhat odd reversal of narrative sequence mentioned earlier, I am of the opinion that, in the absence of a credible explanation from the detectives involved as to the outstanding questions noted in this report, it is difficult to avoid the conclusion that very little of the content of the statement originates with Mr Reed and that there is a strong likelihood that the statement has been fabricated. Even as I write, Mr Reed sits on death row waiting to hear if he will be able to appeal his sentence. I believe he has good grounds to do so.[3]

Statement attributed to James Earl Reed (written out by Detective Hale)

On Monday, May 16th, 1994, I was in Greenville, South Carolina. I had gotten out of Federal Prison in Manchester, Kentucky on April 22nd. I had ridden buses and hitchhiked and ended up in Greenville. I didn't know much about Greenville, but I asked around, ended up in a bad area of town, and bought a gun from a black guy there in Greenville. I paid $45.00 for the gun, which was a silvery-colored, somewhat rusty 9 mm semi-automatic pistol. I don't remember the brand name, but it was a heavy gun. The magazine held 9 rounds and I bought 10 rounds with the gun. The bullets were ball-point rounds. On Monday night I hitch hiked down to Charleston. I caught rides with different people and spent Monday night, Tuesday morning and Tuesday afternoon on the road. I ended up in Charleston at about 6.30 p.m. on May 17th, 1994. When I got in town, I telephoned Barbara Lafayette, who lives in Adams Run. Barbara is the mother of Laurie Camberlen, who is my ex-girlfriend. I had a good conversation with Barbara for 10 or 15 minutes. I told her I was out of prison and that I would drop by some time. I called Barbara from the Circle K store at Highway 17 across from the Mazda dealer. Also a BP Gas Mart is next door. On Tuesday night, I stayed around the Circle K for a while, then I walked to Citadel Mall and walked through the mall for about 2 hours. Then I walked to the shopping center that has Advance Auto Parts, then I went back to the Circle K.

Tuesday night, I slept in the bushes behind Circle K. On Wednesday morning, May 18th, 1994, I left my nylon carry bag, (which contained some personal items) and my jacket in the woods behind the Circle K store. I hitch-hiked to Adams Run on Wednesday. I caught two rides and got there about 1:00 p.m., although I don't know what time it was because I don't have a watch. I went straight to the Lafayette's house. I knocked on the front door, but nobody was there. I got Joseph's coat off the clothesline and waited in the woods behind the house. I went to the house and I wanted to talk to both Barbara and Joseph about the anger and the hurt I felt after spending 2 ½ years in prison. I waited for a few hours, then both Barbara and Joseph pulled up in their small two-door red car. Barbara was driving. She was very surprised to see me. Joseph was non-chalant about seeing me and he shook hands with me, then he went to feed the dog. Barbara opened the door and invited me in. She asked me if I wanted any-thing to drink, but I told her no. We went back to the TV room and Barbara turned on the TV. Barbara sat on the couch and I had a seat in a chair to Barbara's right. Barbara told me that her daughter (Laurie) had remarried and that Laurie's son, J.R., was doing well. He (J.R.) should be 4 ½ years old now. Barbara and I talked for 20 or 30 minutes. Barbara asked why I got out of truck-ing (driving a truck) and I explained that I got out of it because of her daughter, Laurie. I was standing near the entertainment center. I told Barbara that I wanted to explain to her and Joseph how angry I felt after being in prison for 2 ½ years. I told Barbara that I didn't want to make small talk. I asked Joseph to come into the room; he was in the bathroom and he told me he would be there in a minute. At that point I pulled the gun out. I was stand-ing 6 or 7 feet from Barbara facing her. I was holding the gun in my right hand; it was pointing at Barbara. The gun had 10 rounds in it, 9 rounds in the magazine and one round in the chamber. The hammer was cocked and I think the safety lever on the left side of the gun was broken off. I told Barbara "See how angry I am" and gestured at her with the gun. Barbara said something in a panicky voice, and Joseph came out of the bathroom. Joseph said "James, what are you doing?" and he hit the gun with his right hand. My finger was on the trigger. The gun fired and a bulet hit Barbara. I don't know where Barbara was hit first, but the gun kept going off and Barbara was shaking like she was having a seizure as the bullets hit her.

Joseph ran back into the bathroom and I shot at him. He came back
out of the bathroom like he was coming at me and I shot him again.
Suddenly Joseph was on the hallway floor and the slide on the gun
was locked back and it was out of bullets. I picked the shell casings
up off the floor because I was panicky and didn't want the evidence
to lead to me. I put the cases in my right front pants pocket. I ran
into the kitchen and dumped Barbara's purse on the kitchen table
and got Barbara's car keys. As I left the house, Barbara was still sitting on the couch. She was slumped down, her eyes were open, but
she wasn't moving. Joseph was lying in the hallway and he was in
a fetal position and his muscles were twitching. I was too scared to
telephone for help. I went outside and went to the woods and got
Joseph's coat, then I went to their car and drove off. As I drove down
Laurie Street, I drove past four black males and I stopped the car
near them. I did not know any of them. One of them approached
he car and started asking me questions. He was in his late 30's or
early 40's. He was a medium-complexioned, about 5-' 06" to 5-' 08",
and had a medium build. He was asking what was all the shooting
about, what was I doing in their car, etc. I just took off and turned
right onto I74. I drove past the little store on Highway I74 sort of
near the post office in Adams Run. A boy about 16 or 17 named
Cahajah tried to wave me down because he recognized me. I kept
going. I drove straight onto Hwy 164, then onto Hwy 162 towards
Charleston. My intent was to get the hell out of there and drive
to downtown Charleston. I passed two police cars with their blue
lights on and I decided I had to get rid of the car. I turned right off
Highway 162 onto Scott White Road. As I made the first left turn
on Scott White Road, I got the 9 mm casings out of my right front
pocket and threw them out of the window (the passenger window) of
the car. I was looking for a place to ditch the car and I turned down
a little road to the left. I drove the car in behind a tarpaper shack. I
grabbed Joseph's coat and the gun and I got out and started running
towards the woods. I left the keys in the car. There were 2 to 4 guys
standing about 25 yards away. One of them yelled, "Hey, you want
to buy anything?" (meaning buy drugs) and I just answered "No" as
I ran into the woods. I ran through the woods towards 162, then I
followed 162 back towards Charleston. I stayed in the woods where
I could see the road and the vehicles, but hopefully far enough away
so that nobody could see me. Before I crossed Highway 162, I threw
the gun away in the woods. I didn't hide it, I just threw it behind
me. I then ran out to the roadway and saw a tree stump. On the

other side of the road was a driveway with large white rocks, and nearby was a dark wooden fence. A little further down was a white wooden fence. I hitched a ride back to the Circle K on Highway 17 near the Mazda dealership. I got my bag and my coat from behind the Circle K. I hitched aother ride to the Montague Exit off I-26. I walked across to the on-ramp and caught another ride with some-one in a short van and he took me 5 miles down the interstate to another exit, which had a Taco Bell, a Home Depot and a K-Mart. Then I caught another ride up I-26 for about 20 or 30 miles at least. I ended up at a BP Mart and went to the on-ramp and stayed in the woods overnight. Then on Thurdsay morning at about 8:30 a.m. I got arrested by a Dorchester County Sheriff's Deputy. I cooperated and offered no resistance. End of Statement.

Notes

1. It is standard practice throughout most jurisdictions to caution suspects before questioning them. The caution usually takes the form 'You are being arrested on suspicion of ---. You do not have to say anything, but anything you say may be taken down and used against you in a court of law. Do you understand?'
2. Olsson J. (2004). *Forensic Linguistics: An Introduction to Language, Crime and the Law*. Continuum.
3. Mr Reed elected to be executed by electric chair on 20 June 2008. He was therefore a 'volunteer'. In my view he was not competent to make this deci-sion, given the linguistic evidence of his lack of mental powers, and a his-tory of mental illness added to the inevitable depradations of 12 years on death row. On the day before he was executed, a judge in Illinois ruled, in another case, that just because a defendant was competent to stand trial did not mean that defendant was competent to represent themselves, which is what Mr Reed had done after firing his lawyers at his trial in 1996. This rul-ing should have given Supreme Court judges pause for thought in Mr Reed's case, but it did not. An Australian friend, Charles Willock, and myself made representations to the governor right up to the last moment of Mr Reed's life, but we were unsuccessful. Our attempts at mobilizing local media in South Carolina also failed. None of the lawyers I spoke to believed that James Earl Reed was mentally competent to be executed or that he deserved to die. The private investigator who tirelessly fought for James' rights in the last years of his life, Phillip Upton, told me that the prison guards at the death row facil-ity where he was incarcerated before being moved to the death house treated him with unfailing kindness and compassion, mindful of his mental state and his efforts to establish his innocence.

Part 3
16
BETRAYED BY A FULL STOP

Sandra Weddell was a popular mother of three young children. She was well liked in her community, where she belonged to a number of voluntary organizations. A highly qualified nurse, and a person with strong religious beliefs who was widely known for her kindness to others, it came as a shock to her local community to learn that she had, apparently, killed herself. But had she?

Consider the short letter below, the 'suicide' note said to have been left by Mrs Weddell. What is unusual about it? Normally I would not think of asking a reader to do this, but you might like to try transcribing this letter yourself before reading further. You may be surprised at the result.

Garry.

I am typing this note, because I know that if I were to hand write it and leave it for you, then I know that you wouldn't read it.

I am so sorry for all the hurt I have caused you garry. I never meant to hurt you or to cause you so much pain.

I made a stupid mistake and I betrayed your trust, and I betrayed my family at the same time. I don't know what made me do what I did. I wish the whole thing had never happened. It all got out of hand. I have ended up with nothing.

You are kind to want to forgive me. I don't deserve your forgiveness.

When you think of me, just try and think of the happier times.

Sandra Jane Weddell

On the last day in January 2007 in suburban Bedfordshire, not far from London, Garry Weddell, a police inspector, knocked on his neighbour's door and asked him to help find his wife, Sandra. He told the neighbour his wife had been missing since the previous day. After a short time

Sandra Weddell was found dead in the garage of the family home. She had apparently died of asphyxia. A cable tie was found around her neck. Near to the victim's body was a single A4 printed sheet with the above note. On examining the national records on types of murders, police found that all previous deaths involving a cable tie had been murder – there were no suicides. This in itself was not necessarily conclusive, but when the circumstances of the discovery of the body were taken into account, police started to become suspicious.

The candidates for authorship of the 'suicide note' were Sandra Weddell herself and her husband, Garry Weddell. I had worked on a suspicious death case for Bedfordshire Police several years earlier and after the discovery of the body I was asked by the same force to look at the alleged suicide note.

Initially, I made some subjective observations on the text. As the reader will have seen, there is nothing very unusual about the language in the above letter, but observant readers who transcribed the text, as invited, will probably have noticed that after the opening salutation, which is simply 'Garry', there is a full stop. It is such a 'small' detail that several people did in fact fail to notice it. In any case, this full stop turned out to be highly significant, for a number of reasons, which I will go into later.

Another thing you may have noticed is that the writer's name is centred on the page, written as 'Sandra Jane Weddell'. Again, how many of us will have transcribed it as such? Most writers typically print or write their name in the left hand margin, as did almost everyone invited to transcribe the above letter.

At this point we need to take a foray into a branch of linguistics known as *pragmatics*. Linguists use this word to describe how speakers make meaning, sometimes to say more than they mean – but in general *what* they say in order to mean something. In the eighteenth century it might have been common for a wife to sign her name in full when writing to her husband, but in modern times it's very unusual. Why didn't she just write her name 'Sandra'. It's not as if her husband would have said to himself 'I wonder which Sandra could have written this to me'.

Here is another word you will find useful: *prescriptive*. In the context of language it means 'proper' language or 'correct' language, language which follows all the rules or *prescriptions* of grammar. If you look at the letter above you will see that aside from one or two very minor glitches it follows the rules of traditional grammar. There are no grammatical errors in it, unless one were being particularly picky. For example, *garry* is written with a lower case 'g', and there is no comma before *garry*. Other than this, the letter is entirely grammatical. Bear in mind that these minor omissions may be no more than the product of haste, rather than lack of knowledge about the correct forms. So, these points aside, I think we can agree that the letter follows the rules of prescribed grammar.

Now this may not seem very important, but actually it is much rarer than we think. I get letters from people all the time, and in my experience many letters are written with less than perfect grammar. With today's emphasis on communicative competence rather than grammar, many people nowadays have difficulty with issues such as spelling and punctuation.

Other people commented on the oddity of the letter being typed out rather than handwritten. You will have seen the apparent explanation for this: 'I am typing this note, because I know that if I were to hand write it and leave it for you, then I know that you wouldn't read it'. To the extent that this point – typing *vs* writing by hand – concerns motive for an action, it is a psychological question, and hence outside of the linguist's domain. On the other hand, insofar as it concerns the form in which the letter is produced it is a linguistic question, because of something we refer to as *mode*. Strictly speaking *mode* refers to whether language is in the form of speech, writing, dictation and so on. There are several speech modes: speech in casual conversation, language spoken by a teacher to a class, a college or university lecture, the speech of a news reader – this latter being speech which is written in order to be read aloud. Similarly, there are a number of ways of producing written language. We can write out something manually, with a pen or pencil, we can type it on a typewriter, we can use a word processor, and so on. In the course of working as a forensic linguist I have noticed that when the medium changes – for example, handwritten text *vs* word-processed text – there are always a few minor changes in the writer's style. In one case I noticed some changes in a series of letters which I could not explain. The forensic computer expert who also worked on the case later told me that some of the letters had been typed on a laptop while others had come from an office desktop machine. As anybody who has used both will know, laptops are not as convenient to use as conventional desktop machines – the keyboard is smaller, as is the screen and there is usually no mouse. These differences of medium or mode can cause minor changes in style. Given that this was a highly personal letter, and that it could have been written out in less than two minutes, and given the explanation as to why it had not been handwritten, I felt that *mode* was a factor in its authorship.

After considering the content of the letter it seemed that the likeliest candidates for authorship were Sandra Weddell herself and her husband Garry Weddell, the police inspector. Mrs Weddell was a senior nurse in a nearby hospital who also worked part time as an examination invigilator for the local examination authority. She had attended a morning examination session at a local school and had returned home for lunch on 30 January 2007, and was then due to return to the school at approximately 2 p.m. on the same day. From the school she was then due to pick up her own children from another school before returning home at approximately 4 p.m. Mrs Weddell did not return to the examination for the afternoon invigilation session and nor were her children picked up from school. The school called her husband at work and he picked up the children. Mrs Weddell was not found until the next day.

In many forensic cases we have very few examples of the language of candidate authors. In a kidnap case, for example, you might have only one or two letters. People who intend to commit crime are usually careful to commit as little to paper as possible. However, in the present case we had plenty of examples of both writers. In one letter, shortly after his wife's death Garry Weddell wrote:

Please don't send any more letters to any of my family members. They are all just as grief stricken as i am over this matter. We are meeting up regularly to allow me to get what i need to get off my chest. Family support is the best therapy at this time. I have that support in place.

What struck me immediately about this letter was the brevity of the sentences. The average sentence length here is just under 9 words. Looking at the 'suicide' letter we see that the sentence length is not much more than this – just under 12 words. This was a pattern that was to be repeated right across Mr Weddell's letters. Sandra, on the other hand, tended to write quite long sentences. At one point she had to write to her child's school in connection with a lapse in their security arrangements regarding the collection of children after school. She wrote: 'However, on Wednesday 18th January, which is the date that I brought to your attention, Fred[1] was collected by Mr Arbuthnot, who has never collected Fred before and I don't know who handed Fred over on that occasion or indeed why.' This sentence (with names changed to protect the anonymity of others) is over 40 words long. It is not at all unusual for Mrs Weddell to write such long sentences. In fact one of her sentences was over 130 words long. Her average sentence length was nearly double that of her husband's. Moreover, she appeared to have a fondness for commas, dashes and semi-colons, sprinkled somewhat liberally across her letters, and not always with sound grammatical reasons. It was her habit to string whole sentences together, separated by no more than a series of commas.

One question that comes up in the popular media from time to time is the idea of the 'linguistic fingerprint'. According to this idea, each of us has a unique, identifiable way of using language. However, this idea needs to be thought about very carefully. Balanced against the 'fingerprint' idea is the concept of 'individual variation'. What kinds of factors might contribute to variation in our writing style? Above, I referred to *mode*, the form in which language is produced, and I said that depending on whether we hand write a text, type it on a desktop or a laptop, or write it on a blackboard using chalk, that these different methods and environments of production, would probably produce differences in our style of language use. But, in addition to mode, there are a number of other factors which could increase how much variation an author shows. I will first describe these, and then I will relate this question of variation to the texts in this case – both those of the victim Sandra Weddell and her husband, Garry Weddell.

- *Vocabulary*: We use different vocabularies (also called 'lexicons') depending on who we are writing to, what we are saying, and what the circumstances are of the communication. Formal letters will contain very precise words which are usually absent from informal communications. When writing to someone we know, for example, we would probably be informal, but when writing to a stranger the opposite would apply. A report would probably use technical vocabulary, while – by contrast – a birthday card would use very general, common vocabulary.
- *Time*: Another factor likely to produce variation in someone's style of language is the time lapse between two communications. Over a period our vocabulary changes, and so do other factors, like sentence length, phraseology and so on. The longer the period between any two texts, the more likely we are to find differences.
- *Personal circumstances*: A number of changes in our circumstances can produce changes in our use of language, such as bereavement, changes in employment, marriage, having children and so on. Some of these changes can have catastrophic effects on the way we write – and I am not referring to handwriting, though that too can be affected.

- *Cultural changes*: Our culture is changing all the time, though we do not usually notice the differences on a day-to-day basis. As a result of these changes words come and go, old phrases sometimes fall out of fashion, and new ones come along. One area in which you can particularly notice changes is in the way people text on mobile phones – the famous abbreviations, for example, '4u' for 'for you' are now no longer as startling as they first were. Mobile phone texting has continued to evolve, so that we can now easily pick out differences from 4 or 5 years ago. Thus, young texters used to be content with writing 'know' as 'no', but they now frequently write 'na', and for many texters 'dinner' became 'dinna' and has now become 'dina'. Frequently, letters which can be taken for granted are omitted, for example, 'remember' becomes 'remeba'. Even the word 'texting' has modified from 'txtn' to 'txn', for example, 'i ws txn u ls nyt' (I was texting you last night).

Hence, as we can see from the above, there are many reasons why an individual writer's use of language can vary. When we add these possible causes of variation up, they are referred to as **within author variation**. But what about how authors vary from each other?

If two authors have similar backgrounds, similar levels of education, come from the same geographical area, and have similar occupations, then the possibility is that they will not vary much from each other. Conversely, if two authors have widely different social backgrounds, with one being educated to a high level while the other's education was somewhat limited, if they come from different geographical areas, and have completely different types and levels of occupation or profession – then the chances are they will probably have different styles of language use. Collectively, these different social factors are referred to as **inter-author variation**.

So, on the one hand we have within author variation and on the other hand we have inter-author variation.

What makes the linguistic fingerprint idea difficult is this: suppose for a moment we have an inquiry where one of the authors is showing a lot of within author variation, and suppose also that there is very little inter-author variation across the different authors? Then it will be clear that finding significant differences between these different authors would be very difficult.

So, how do these observations relate to the alleged suicide letter, and the letters written by Sandra Weddell and Garry Weddell?

In the present case, some factors do contribute to variation. For example, not all of the texts for each author are of the same type, or written to the same addressee. Some of Mr Weddell's texts are emails, some are letters written in a reporting style, and some of them are business letters. Among his letters there was also one personal email, to a relative.

With regard to Mrs Weddell's texts there was a variety of addressees and text types. However, there are no personal communications among Mrs Weddell's known texts, and since the alleged suicide note can be considered to be a personal communication this could be a complicating factor in assessing her style.

An interesting question that comes up from time to time is that of 'convergence of style'. Do married couples tend to adopt each other's language habits over the years? Again, this will depend on early influences on their language to a large degree: if they are of similar ages and backgrounds then there might already be strong similarities. However, I have seen no evidence that married couples start to write like each other, in terms of the language they use. They might, over the years, adopt some of each other's phrases in speech and other speech habits, but merging written language styles is another question altogether. From what I could see of Sandra's language style there was no evidence that she wrote like Garry, or that Garry wrote like her, even though the couple had been married for a number of years.

In fact, despite the possible sources of variation referred to above, it is noticeable that some basic features of the texts of each author are quite consistent. Whoever Sandra Weddell is writing to, she tends to use the same kind of concatenated, rambling sentence structure as we saw above, and – similarly – whoever Garry Weddell is writing to, we see that he always seems to use short, sharp sentences. In this respect he is like a typical company executive or other senior official – say what you want and get it over with, no messing about, no wandering off the point.

The important point is that these characteristics are found across all of the letters: short sharp sentences for Garry, long, rambling sentences for Sandra. No matter the type of communication each is writing, this is what we find.

After that I reported my findings to the police. They had other evidence as well and arrested Garry Weddell in June 2007.

Tragically, Mr Weddell was given bail and told to keep clear of the area where his relatives lived. However, he appears to have felt vengeful to some of his relatives and, apparently, shot his mother-in-law, Traute Maxfield, before shooting himself. These were the coroners' findings in March, 2008. There seems little doubt that he had killed his wife and then tried to fabricate her suicide.

There is one further interesting detail about the full stop after the word 'Garry' in the opening line of the letter. Forensic scientists had to test the ink on the letter, to see if it was compatible with that found in the printer attached to the family computer. In order to do this they had to remove a sample of the ink from the letter. The sample they chose to remove was – the full stop! Fortunately, they had taken very good photographs of the letter before doing so, but even so, I sometimes wonder whether the defence team would have made anything of this point if the case had come to trial.

Note

1. Names changed.

17

A BLAND PAEDOPHILE

It sometimes happens that I am asked to make a comparison between two sets of letters or emails and on looking at the documents I find myself completely stumped for something constructive to say – for the simple reason that the suspect's language style appears, on first sight, to be completely featureless. This happened some years ago in the case of a businessman who was accused of downloading child pornography images from the internet. A highly educated, intelligent man in his fifties, one would not have expected him to be a person who made basic mistakes, but people do unexpected things. His mistake was that, on finding the photos and images he had downloaded from a certain website, which were not to his liking, he wrote a letter of complaint to the company providing the pornography service.

The police do not normally give information out about their sources, but I am led to believe that it was the company that, rather than refunding him his money as he requested, informed the police – anonymously one imagines – that Mr Sowerby had been downloading illegal material. Mr Sowerby was duly visited at rather an early hour in the morning several weeks later and his computer was seized. The offending images were found, as was a copy of the letter of complaint. Mr Sowerby's defence was that the images had been downloaded by a friend of his, who had – unknown to Mr Sowerby – also used his credit card to pay for the transaction. Asked about the letter of complaint Mr Sowerby said that his friend must have panicked when he realized that he, Mr Sowerby, would eventually notice the transaction. Thinking to get the money returned to his account, the friend had obviously concocted the letter of complaint. Asked to name the 'friend' Mr Sowerby named a local plumber who, however, had recently died. What could not be argued was that the plumber and Mr Sowerby had been acquainted. However, inquiries revealed that none of the plumber's friends or family believed that he knew how to use a computer, especially with regard to the sending and receiving of emails, making payments over the internet, or being able to download pictures or videos. What was more, nobody in the plumber's family recalled him as being much of a letter writer. It was generally felt that he was at best semi-literate. Eventually, however, examples of the plumber's correspondence were obtained and these, with the other relevant texts in the case are given below:

Text Sample 1: First email in child pornography case (questioned text)

I have spent some time this evening at your site and have not been able to access any material of the type that was used to advertise it. It was a bit like memory lane. Some of the material was lifted straight from 35mm films and videos that I watched 20 years ago. Seriously, though, it really was nothing like the preview and I have no wish to subscribe to this type of site. Please would you give me access to the type of material promised or cancel the charge to my card.

Incidentally, I had no trouble with the foto archive but what is one supposed to do with New CamsVideo and Erotic Show sections? I was unable to get anything from them.

This was the email that was found on Mr Sowerby's home computer and which he attributed to the plumber. As to general language ability it seemed to be in some contrast to the known writings of the plumber:

Text Sample 2: Known example of plumber's correspondence

Dear Mr Brown, Please could you contact me as soon as possible as to my situation at the moment and why I am being keep here at the prison. And when will I be released as not knowing is worse of all. I hope to see you soon.

The above example shows a number of basic prescriptive errors, including 'being keep' instead of 'being kept' and the termination of a sentence before 'and'. In addition, the plumber confuses the superlative with the comparative adjective, that is, he writes 'worse' instead of 'worst'. He thus appears to exhibit difficulties of three different types: grammar, punctuation and lexis (vocabulary). On the surface, at least, his writing is not easily comparable to that of the email found on Mr Sowerby's computer. The businessman on the other hand, demonstrates a somewhat greater competence, as can be seen from the following text:

Text Sample 3: Known example of businessman's correspondence

On Tuesday 1 May 2001, my wife and I went out to dinner with my daughter and her partner. When I returned home, at about 01.30 there were two messages on the answerphone. One was from the central station, that monitors the alarm at Greenlake Street, Smithville, informing me that the telephone connection to the premises had failed. The second was from my PA, Mrs Jones who is an alternate key holder at Greenlake Street, to the effect that she had been informed of the line failure, had attended the premises but found no indication of anything amiss. I returned the call to the monitoring station and learned that the probable cause was a line fault and that the incident had been 'policed' (log 101 timed at 22.35) and that the police had attended and reported the premises to be secure.

I began by looking for signs of markedness in the different known texts. At first sight, Mr Sowerby's texts seemed to be very formal, perhaps even pretentious in parts. However, at this stage this is just an impression and needs to be tested. In his survey of markedness as a linguistic topic, Battistella (1996) notes that the relative frequency of a construction is an accurate indicator of markedness *vs.* unmarkedness. In other words, the rarer a construction is, the more likely it is to be marked. Some forms of markedness are purely stylistic, for example, the use of excessive repetition. As such, they are hard to measure and can only be used for an impressionistic account of authorship. In the present instance I decided to take an internet and corpus survey of the phrases found in the known and questioned texts, and test them for frequency. All of the phrases were surveyed on a major internet search engine and a sample of these were re-checked using the British National Corpus (BNC), compiled by scholars at Oxford University. Further checking of some of the samples was done using another corpus of language, the Cobuild corpus, compiled by scholars at Birmingham University.

I found that the best way to search for instances of markedness was to print out a copy of the text and underline as many phrases as possible. I aimed to do approximately one phrase of three to five words in length for every ten words of text. Some phrases, because of narrowness of context, were just not suitable, especially those containing proper nouns and personalized or coded references. It was important to avoid sample bias by just selecting what appeared unusual or marked.

After I had selected the phrases to search for, I then looked for alternative ways of saying or writing those phrases. I would usually change only one feature at a time – while attempting to keep to the text's register, that is, if the text was formal or businesslike, then I tried to ensure that any changes reflected this. An example from Mr Sowerby's known text is shown in Table 17.1. In the Table 17.1 we see an excerpt from Mr Sowerby's letter, the phrase '. . . the probable cause was . . .' As a noun 'cause' is fairly rare when compared with its presence as a verb. You

Table 17.1. Example from Mr Sowerby's known text

Textual phrase	Alternatives
the probable cause was	the cause was probably probably caused by probably because

Table 17.2. Examples of known text markedness

Phrase	Search engine (Global)	Search engine (UK)	BNC	Markedness
the one which	1,150,000	401,000	244	
the one that	26,000,000	1,150,000	1,030	Unmarked
the cause was probably	505	1,220	0	
the probable cause was	10,800	373	1	Marked
probably caused by	1,070,000	117,000	1	
of anything amiss	566	351	1	Marked
of anything wrong	28,500	10,500	1	

Note: Mr Sowerby's text choices are indicated here in **bold** type.

can verify this by searching the internet with different constructions. In addition, the adverb 'probably' is much more common than the adjective 'probable'.[1] This is attested on Google, Cobuild and BNC. Thus, what we find from the phrase 'the probable cause was', is that it contains two marked items, relative to the items in the text. Of the two alternatives 'probably caused by' is by far the most frequent of the three possibilities given here. The next step was to check frequencies for each selected phrase and the alternatives I was able to devise. Again, it was important not to choose only those examples which seemed marked. Usually I would compile a table as shown in Table 17.2.

I then looked at the known text of the plumber and found that, typically, his marked structures were to do with prescriptive data, largely spelling, but also grammatical, for example, 'being keep' instead of 'being kept', 'worse of all' instead of 'worst of all'. These types of error are also marked and can be quantified using corpora and search engines (though compilers of corpora tend to 'tidy' up text and thus suppress errors). I found no examples of marked phrases, as shown in Table 17.3. The questioned text also contained a number of marked constructions, as examples in Table 17.4 show.

The next step was to compile a comparative table of types of markedness, as shown in Table 17.5. As can be seen from Table 17.5, the

Table 17.3. Phrases from the plumber's texts

Phrase	Search engine (Global)	Search engine (UK)	BNC	Markedness
contact me	66,400,000	1,530,000	180	Unmarked
get in touch with me	1,020,000	115,000	1	
as to my situation	282,000	7	0	Unmarked
about my situation	175,000	9,130	1	
on returning home	155,000	44,600	1	Unmarked
on coming home	49,200	3,290	1	

Table 17.4. Examples of questioned text markedness

Phrase	Search engine (Global)	Search engine (UK)	BNC	Markedness
material of the type	93,500	2,790	0	Marked
type of material	1,180,000	148,000	1	
it really was nothing like	24,600	2	0	Marked
it was nothing like	170,000	14,600	1	
I have no wish to subscribe	3	2	205 ('no wish to')	Marked
I do not wish to subscribe	18,100	1,910	255 ('do not wish to')	

Note: The author's text choices are indicated here in **bold** type.

Table 17.5. Type and density of markedness

	Lexical	Grammatical	Categorial	Competence	Density
K (Businessman)	'probable', 'cause', 'amiss', 'to the effect that'	'reported the premises to be' [construction], 'anything amiss', [word order]	Nominalization: 'cause', 'effect'		0.05
K (Plumber)				'being keep', 'worse of all'	0.04
Questioned	'access' *vs.* 'get', 'obtain'	'not able to access', 'that was used' [passive]; 'material of the type'	Nominalization: 'wish'		0.04

density of marked constructions and unmarked constructions found in the texts is roughly the same across both known authors and the questioned author. However, the second known author, the plumber, exhibits a completely different type of marked construction when compared with that of the businessman. Mr Sowerby's text is, with respect to the type of markedness shown, as well as its register, much more like the questioned text. On the other hand, the plumber's issues of markedness relate to competence in use of the language. In my report I concluded that it was highly likely that of the two candidates, the questioned email originated from the businessman, not the plumber. Put simply, the plumber was more or less semi-literate, while the businessman was highly educated. The differences in their known texts reflected this, and the similarity between Mr Sowerby's known writings and the complaint email were much greater than any similarity between that of the deceased plumber's letters and the complaint email. This evidence was submitted to the court, at which point the businessman pleaded guilty to downloading and possessing child pornographic images. He escaped a jail sentence but was placed on the sex offender's register for 10 years.

Note

1. The word 'cause' frequently co-occurs with the word 'probable'.

18

PROSECUTOR MEMO LEADS TO ABUSE OF PROCESS RULING

Mary Smith[1] states that she was driving her car down a two-way street through the town of Chawborough when, owing to a temporary distraction she swerved and went over the central dividing line. A police officer was in a patrol car behind her and responded by signalling her to stop.

It appeared to the officer that Ms Smith's breath smelled of alcohol, so he requested Ms Smith to accompany him to the police vehicle where he could breathalyse her. She got into the back of the police vehicle and was handed the mouthpiece. However, despite several attempts she was not successful in giving a satisfactory sample. As a result, the officer arrested Ms Smith and took her to Chawborough police station where the breathalysing process was again attempted, but this time using the station equipment, known as a Lion Intoxilyzer 6000. Again, Ms Smith failed to provide a sample. According to the officers several attempts were made to breathalyse Ms Smith, but she was not co-operative. According to Ms Smith she was unable to provide a sample because she was hyperventilating and in a state of panic.

The officers charged Ms Smith with the offence of failing to provide a sample. This is even more serious than being charged with drunken driving.

The case came to the Chawborough magistrates' court and was heard in front of three lay magistrates. The alternative in the United Kingdom for some hearings of this kind is that the case is heard before a district judge (previously known as a 'stipendiary magistrate'). In this case, however, the case came before the magistrates.

Among the evidence tended by the prosecution were two statements from the two officers who had attempted to breathalyse Ms Smith. Prior to the trial the defending barrister was struck by the similarity between the two police statements, excerpts of which are given below:

Excerpt from Statement 1
I wish to state in relation to this matter that throughout my dealings with X she . . . was not complaining of any problems regarding

her breathing . . . and was not showing any non-verbal signs to suggest this. In my opinion X did not have any form of panic attack or hyperventilation throughout.

Excerpt from Statement 2
X did not in my presence complain of any problems regarding her breathing, nor any non-verbal signs in relation to the breath procedure . . . X did not have any kind of panic attack or hyperventilation.

The barrister questioned the first police officer as to the similarities. The officer maintained that the similarity was purely coincidental. Asked if he could account for this 'co-incidence' the officer replied that he could not. Asked if he had shown his own statement to the second officer, the first officer said he had not and that there was no possibility that the second officer could have seen his, the first officer's statement. The barrister was nothing if not determined. He pressed the officer for a satisfactory answer. Eventually, the officer said the only thing he could think of which might account for the similarity was a memo he had received from the prosecutor. The barrister asked him what memo he was referring to, pointing out that no memo had been disclosed to the defence. This was slightly disingenuous of the barrister as it is not usual for prosecutor's memos to be disclosed.

The officer reiterated that he had received a memo from the prosecutor. The defence barrister requested the court to ask the prosecutor to disclose the memo. The prosecutor said he was unaware of any memo. He appeared to look through the bundle of documents in front of him but could apparently find no memo. The defence barrister offered to help him. This offer was declined, but the chair of the bench then asked if perhaps the witness could look through the bundle since he would surely recognize the memo more easily. The bundle of prosecutor documents was handed to the police officer as he stood at the witness box and he immediately found the memo. The memo was copied and all parties were given a copy.

The memo purported to be a request from the prosecutor to the disclosure officer to make disclosure of several items which the defence required in order to run the case. This list included the mouthpiece, any notes the officers may have made in the course of Ms Smith's detention at the police station and, crucially, a request to the officers to provide Section 9 statements (i.e. witness statements) on the breathalysing process as it had applied to Ms Smith. These were the statements upon which the defence barrister was examining the officer when the fact of the memo's existence was first mentioned.

However, the memo was extremely derogatory to the defendant and her legal representatives, and in fact represented the task of collecting this evidence as a 'pain' – effectively a nuisance to the officers and the prosecution.

The defence immediately took issue with the memo and requested permission from the court for an adjournment so that an expert could be called to look at the memo and the two statements. This adjournment and the request for an expert was immediately granted by the bench.

The memo was given to me to look at, along with the two statements. Here is an excerpt of the memo:

Excerpts from the Prosecutor's Memo
. . . Enclosed is a copy of a defence case statement received from the defendant's solicitor (a lot of nonsense in a vain attempt to avoid the inevitable) which sadly we have to respond to.

I will need section 9 statements from PC Smith and yourself that the lady was not suffering from any form of panic attack or hyperventilation. If you can detail what qualifications you have to operate the procedure and how often and how many procedures you have conducted it may help. I want to show you are an experienced operator.

The question of whether or not you acted unreasonably in not allowing the lady the opportunity to try again or to provide a blood sample can be dealt with at the trial. Please be prepared to deal with the question.

I know all this is a pain but I fear these solicitors will try anything to get their desperate client off the hook . . .

Having carried out an analysis of the documents I made the following observations:

1.   The memo does not appear to be a request for a disclosure, but a demand for the disclosure to follow the prosecutor's prescription. For example, the memo requests the officers to provide statements 'that Ms Smith was not suffering from any form of hyperventilation or panic attack'. I considered that this was not an objective, impartial request, but a direction to the officers to state 'that Ms Smith was not suffering from any form of hyperventilation', and so on. Similarly, the memo asks the officer to provide details of his experience in operating the breathalyser equipment, but this is also phrased as a demand. The

prosecutor says 'I want to show you are an experienced operator [of this equipment]'. However, at the time of writing there was no way that the prosecutor could have known if this were true or not. The memo also contains a presumption of the doctor's findings: 'Can I have an explanation as to why the doctor was called to rebut the defence assertion that it was due to the "shock/hyperventilation".' The linguist considered that this is really a question followed by a statement of intent: (i) Can I have an explanation as to why the doctor was called? And (ii) there is a purposive infinitive 'to', which can be rendered as '[in order to] rebut the defence assertion that it was due to . . . hyperventilation'. In other words, properly parsed, the memo appeared to say: 'Can I have an explanation as to why the doctor was called [because I wish] to rebut the defence assertion that . . .' The legal view was that the prosecutor should not have disclosed the defence's arguments to the officer because the officer was also a witness. The linguistic view was that the prosecutor was informing the officer of how he intended to counter the defence case, but also that he had apparently done so in a confusing and ambiguous way which could have been designed to obscure this fact from the officer's notice.

2.   In this memo the prosecutor also tells the officer that he should expect questioning regarding the issue of whether he, the officer, acted unreasonably in refusing to allow the defendant the opportunity to give another sample.

3.   In addition, the prosecutor also gives the officer unnecessary information regarding defence disclosure.

4.   Finally, the memo talks about the defendant and her defence team in the most disparaging and insulting terms, and, effectively, invites the police officer – who, it must be recalled – is a witness to the alleged offence – to share this view. For example, he writes: 'Enclosed is a copy of a defence case statement received from the defendant's solicitor (a lot of nonsense in a vain attempt to avoid the inevitable) which sadly we have to respond to'. There are several points at issue: (i) the prosecutor should not, unless under exceptional circumstances, be disclosing a defence case statement to a witness. Regrettably, the officer is not only a witness he is also the disclosure officer. This, it was claimed, is not best practice; (ii) at the linguistic level, the prosecutor uses inclusive 'we', thus inviting the officer to share his view that the defence case is 'nonsense' and hence that the task of collecting the evidence is a nuisance. Added to the unnecessary information the prosecutor gives the officer in connection with the defence arguments and evidence, this invites the officer to take

a hostile attitude to the defence and forewarns him how the defence will be run, possibly creating an opportunity for tainting his evidence.

The trial was reconvened at the Chawborough magistrates' court in front of the same bench as before. I was called and asked to comment on the memo. I outlined the arguments in my report and I was examined and cross-examined on them. There was no prior examination on my admissibility as a witness because the prosecution had not objected to a linguist appearing.

I explained the linguistic issues, which were as follows:

1.   A linguistic analysis of the memo was valid because (i) it is not only what we say that counts, but the context in which we say it. Thus, it might not be wrong for the prosecutor, if having a conversation with a colleague (who was not also a witness) to exclaim privately out of ear-shot from any of the parties that 'the defence case is a lot of nonsense'. Also, it would not be wrong for the prosecutor, if cross-examining the defendant, to say 'Madam, that is a lot of nonsense' or to say to the bench, 'Sir, in my view the defence case is a lot of nonsense'. However, the prosecutor was writing to a witness in the case, and was inviting that witness to share his view, with the use of inclusive 'we'. This is the second linguistic point: speakers can include or exclude others by the use of 'we'. In the present case both the prosecutor and the witness have certain duties which they have to carry out under the law. This is certainly a valid use of 'we'. However, the prosecutor went beyond the strict allocation of functions to the witness and invited him to share a derogatory, partial, view which was – crucially (in terms of prosecutorial codes of conduct) – anything but dispassionate. A prosecutor may have contact with a witness prior to a trial, but in his/her dealings with a witness must be dispassionate. This applies particularly to comments about a defendant. The prosecutor must not contaminate a case by commenting on such matters to a witness.

2.   I also claimed that the way in which the prosecutor requested the evidence hardly constituted a request, but was in effect a demand for the presentation of evidence in a particular way. This applied to the 'that' clause previously referred to, and to the officer's status as an 'experienced operator'. Nobody disputed that the officer was probably experienced, but the prosecutor should have been more circumspect in his phrasing, saying for example 'Could you please provide me with any information as to your experience as an operator of this equipment' or, even more

plainly, 'What is your experience as an operator?' In court the linguist claimed that the prosecutor's sentence 'I want to show you are an experienced operator' was the equivalent of a leading question. Few judges or magistrates would allow counsel to say something like, 'Constable X, tell us about your qualifications with this breathalysing equipment because I would like to show the court you are an experienced operator.'

3.   It was also noted that the prosecutor, by using deprecating language to an official who was, in the sphere of such issues as 'chain of command' an inferior functionary, and therefore not at liberty to contradict the prosecutor, effectively put the officer under pressure. This was, in a manner of speaking, the equivalent of a junior employee having to laugh at a boss's racist or sexist jokes. All of these points together, it was claimed, meant that the officer was under pressure to conform to a set of instructions in a particular way, and was not free to gather his evidence in an impartial, objective manner.

4.   The defence asked whether the close lexical and phrasing similarities across the two statements showed causation, in the sense that the statements – which used some of the same phrases as the memo and a number of phrases which were identical to each other (one or two of which were very rare phrases) must have been influenced by the memo. I replied that I felt there were strong similarities, but that causation here was a legal issue, rather than a linguistic one, but that insofar as *both* witness statements followed the structure and wording of the memo, there were strong grounds for believing that the language of the memo had influenced the language and structure of the statements.

It should be noted that the prosecuting attorney in this 'failure to provide a specimen' charge was not the same prosecutor who had written the memo.

The prosecutor raised several very interesting points:

1.   He pointed out (in the form of 'Wouldn't you agree with me . . .') that the fact that the statements contained many similar phrases could be attributed to the fact that police officers speak and write in a 'jargon-like' manner, that is, that they use police register.
2.   He stated that, since police officers are a hardworking community, it was quite reasonable that an officer witness could also be a disclosure officer in a case. He suggested that police officers can make up their own minds about such matters and would not necessarily be liable to influence.

I felt that these were good arguments but I could not wholly subscribe to them:

A.   It is true that practitioners of different professions develop a kind of jargon or register, and this is particularly true of members of highly institutionalized professions such as police officers. Nevertheless, this could not explain the joint occurrence of several phrases of more than six words in length, as well as one or two very unusual phrases, for example, 'non-verbal signs'. The officer who had appeared on the witness stand had not used the phrase 'non-verbal signs', but had spoken of 'body language'. Moreover, there was a very high common lexical content between the two statements.

B.   Of course I could have no comment on the propriety or otherwise of witnesses acting as disclosure officers, since this was an operational or even a legal point rather than a linguistic one. Nor could I comment on whether police officers are any more able or not able to make up their own minds regarding their views of a case, a defendant in a case, or that defendant's legal representatives. However, I did point out that we had a memo, that the memo was written in certain terms, and that the statements follow the structure of the memo almost precisely, that they contain many similar and identical phrases, and that the two statements are so like each other as to make the probability of their having been independently produced exceedingly low.

Following the linguist's evidence the defence requested that they be able to file a motion for abuse of process. Defence described how the question is laid out in the Police and Criminal Evidence Act, 1984 (Section 78). This section allows the exclusion of evidence if the result would mean unfairness to a defendant. The defence barrister argued that admission of the police statements would contradict the provisions of Section 78, and would result in an unfair trial. This provides that officials cannot abuse their rôle in a prosecution and, crucially, that they cannot act in 'bad faith'. The Code for Crown Prosecutors states that prosecutors 'must be fair, independent and objective', that they should provide 'guidance and advice to investigators' and that they have a duty to put 'all relevant evidence . . . before the court'. However, prosecutors 'should . . . tell . . . police if they believe that some additional evidence may strengthen the case'. An important phase in the decision process of whether to go forward with a case is the evidential stage. A crucial aspect of this is the way in which evidence is gathered. This is because the court can apply a number of rules to test whether evidence should be excluded or not. When considering an application under Section 78, the court will first consider how the evidence was obtained. A breach does not automatically entail exclusion of evidence. Rather, the breach has to be 'significant and substantial'.

In R vs. Derby Crown Court, *ex parte* Brooks, Lord Ormond defined abuse of process as a case where 'the prosecution have manipulated or misused the process of the court so as to deprive the defendant of a protection provided by law . . .'

In reality, the granting of an abuse of process is a rare legal event. According to Dilhorne, in DPP vs. Humphrys (1977), proceedings are stayed only 'in exceptional circumstances'. This comment was echoed by Lord Lane when he was Attorney General in 1990, while Lord Justice Stuart-Smith noted that 'it is a power that should only be exercised sparingly'. One Canadian decision noted that in order for a stay to be granted 'the fundamental principles of justice which underlie the community's sense of fair play and decency' would have to be violated.

In the present case the issue was whether misconduct which undermines the rule of law had taken place, and whether this in turn would constitute an affront to justice.

The prosecution countered by claiming that any such issue could be dealt with in the course of the trial, and that the memo, though clumsily worded, was not an abuse of process because there was no way of knowing what effect it had on the officers' conduct. He also claimed to quote case law stating that an abuse of process ruling to exclude evidence could only be granted if the evidence had not yet been adduced. Since, however, the officer had already begun his evidence, it could not be applied in the present instance.

Defence was able to respond to these points and to put the memo in a much stronger light, especially given the linguistic analysis. He reiterated the previously mentioned linguistic points about context, inclusive 'we', declarative demands and embedded multiple implicatures. He pointed out, as did the justices' clerk, that prosecution was not correct to say that evidence could only be excluded before it was given, since this would in itself violate natural justice.

The magistrates considered the application over a 2 to 3 hour period, and were able to avail themselves of the services of the justices' clerk in the matter. On returning to the court they ruled that the memo had abused the trial process and that an affront to justice had occurred. The case was dismissed and costs were awarded to the defendant, Ms Smith.

This is a significant ruling for forensic linguistics for a number of reasons. First, it is believed to be the first time that linguistic evidence has been given in an abuse of process case. What was demonstrated with this case is that when we speak or write we also *act*. If we are in a position of power we can get others to act. Therefore, to consider the memo as harmless would be to miss the fact that language is action, and – in this case – that it is a type of action which causes other actions. If those actions are illegal or unethical, then it is the causative action to which we should first turn our attention.

In Ms Smith's case I have no idea whether she was inebriated while driving. I would, of course, hope that that was not the case. It is possible that if the prosecutor had not been quite so zealous the police would have been able to win the case and Ms Smith would have been convicted of driving while under the influence of alcohol. I felt that the prosecutor had been overly enthusiastic in this case, and in doing so had managed to hinder the police in their work; a careless use of language from a person in power had derailed what had perhaps been a perfectly sound prosecution case.

Note

1. At the request of the defence barrister in this case personal names and place names have been changed. If this case is featured in subsequent editions of law books, for example, Blackstone's, then this document will be revised to enable readers to refer to the case more formally.

19

LETTERS FROM ANONYMOUS

Mary Smythe was a woman in her forties who had the mental age of a 12-year-old. Friendly and outgoing she was popular with her mother's neighbours in the northern town of Moorheed. Unfortunately, her friendliness seems to have been her downfall because one day she returned home to complain that an elderly male neighbour had sexually assaulted or raped her. Several of her neighbours had indeed seen her going into Joe Brown's house, but they would have had difficulty in believing that the elderly cat-loving Mr Brown would do such a thing. Nevertheless, the matter was reported to the police and Mr Brown was interviewed. Eventually, charges were laid against him. Soon afterwards the neighbours who had reported seeing Mary enter his house on the day of the alleged attack began to receive malicious and threatening letters. They reported receipt of these letters to the police. Other individuals, who were not witnesses, knew of several visits by the victim to the suspect's house, or knew of other information which was damaging to the suspect, or perceived by him to be damaging. These people also received anonymous letters. All of the anonymous letters contained claims, supposedly made by a 'friend' of the suspect, that he, the suspect did not rape the victim.

At about the same time Joe Brown himself wrote several letters to a number of the witnesses and others, effectively making the same claims as the questioned author/s, and in very similar language. Below are some examples of the language of both text groups, the known (K) and the questioned (U). There are two known examples (K1 and K2) and two unknown examples (U1 and U2).

Text Sample 1: Witness intimidation case: Text K1 (Known 1)
    . . . I was arrested and charged with the rape of Mary. I could not believe this as I am and was impotent.

Text Sample 2: Witness intimidation case: Text K1 (Known 2)
    . . . when I was arrested, I was firstly charged with raping Mary, I stated to the Police that I could not rape anyone, as I was impotent, and had been since 1996.

Text Sample 3: Witness intimidation case: Text U1 (Unknown 1)

The good fortune is Joe was able through solicitors, police Forensics and medical experts to prove 100% that he could not and did not rape or have unlawful sex, through his being Impotent and is and has been for five years or more.

Text Sample 4: Witness intimidation case: Text U2 (Unknown 2)

Neither would have known that Joe, was to enter hospital to have tests to Proving that he is and was impotent.

Application of 'markedness'

The reader will have observed a number of references to 'impotent' in both K and U text excerpts. These are abstracted into Table 19.1. What I find curious about these examples is the tense inversion: the projecting clauses ('I could not believe', 'Neither would know') are in the past tense, but the main clause verb is in the present tense. This is a marked structure since (i) it is more usual to cite events in their chronological order, that is, earlier event before later event and (ii) the projecting clauses ('I could not believe' etc) themselves are in the past tense, and it would be more usual that the event nearer the projecting tense in time is mentioned first. The only possible exception is K2 'as I was impotent and had been since 1996' which is no more unusual than '~as I had been impotent since 1996 and was still impotent~'. This example aside, some readers may consider this to be an issue of historical present tense usage. It is certainly true that the narrator in each case may be simply emphasizing the current 'impotence' of the subject. However, this is perhaps a narrative matter rather than a syntactic or semantic matter. Furthermore, the positioning of the present tense within two past tense events in this way does not suggest the historical present tense, at least not in this context.

Table 19.1. References to impotence in K and U texts

Text	Projecting clause	Projected clause
K1	I could not believe this	as I am and was impotent
K2	I could not rape anyone	as I was impotent and had been since 1996
U1	Joe was able . . . to prove . . . that he could not and did not rape . . .	through his being Impotent and is and has been for five years or more
U2	Neither would know that Joe	that he is and was impotent

I suggest, rather, that it is a marked form of some kind. It is not syntactic, since there is no grammatical rule that would specify a chronological sequence in this context. Similarly, it is not a matter of 'non-standardness', since, again, there is no generally accepted standard that we could turn to and say, 'This clause violates a known standard'. What we appear to have is simply an uncommon or unusual formulation rather than a non-standard one. To test this we need to consider some form of language frequency measurement, in such instruments as language corpora or, failing that, a suitable internet search engine. The corpus I used, the BNC[1] corpus, gave the results for these configurations as shown in Table 19.2. This result is not surprising for a corpus result, because corpora are often geared to higher register texts than the examples we see here. Such texts generally reflect a higher percentage of nominalized constructions than informal texts. This can be fairly easily tested if we measure frequencies for determiners such as 'the' and 'a/an'. The percentage of these words in higher register texts, such as academic papers, novels and news media articles is greater than it is in less formal texts, such as letters, emails and other similar texts. The same corpus, the BNC corpus, for example, found only 267 instances of 'you and me' and no more than 564 instances of 'you and I' – and this is on a base of 100 million words. This clearly suggests that the corpus is much more formal in its register stock than, for example, the internet would be. Hence, since the corpus had nothing to offer in the present instance I turned to the internet.

We should be cautious about the use of search engines for a number of reasons. Because of the way search engines work we cannot rely on the exact frequencies given. Most will say, for example, 'about 1,360,000 results'. The 'about' here is significant. The search engine server decides how much time to allot to the search, depending on its current workload. It then reports what it found in the given time on the servers that were most readily available to it. This is why internet searches vary in frequency. However, we can certainly get a very good idea of frequencies, even if we cannot depend on a precise number. Bear in mind, though,

Table 19.2. Corpus results for phrases like 'am and was'

String	Frequency
was and is	60
is and was	2
am and was	1 (two clauses)
was and am	0

that the results you get have to be very significant to be used at all, for example, 10,000 *vs.* 50 is a lot more valid than 10,000 *vs.* 9,000. Where you cannot use a corpus but have to use the internet, for example, if you are searching for a function word, try to triangulate your results using different constructions.

One search engine[2] gives the following counts for various versions of *pronoun + be (present) + be (past)*, and *pronoun + be (past) + be (present)* (see Table 19.3). From these measurements we see that the past–present formulation is much more frequent than the present–past formulation. There appears to be a strong tendency for the past tense verb to precede the present tense verb. Even if we cannot be sure of the precision of search engine frequencies, the search still seems valid, given that the search has been widened to test other pronouns than the ones we are interested in. In addition, I suggest that intuition tells us that the past–present sequence is more typical than the present–past sequence, and also that if we are projecting ('I thought', 'he said', 'I believed' etc) in the past tense then it would be more usual to refer to the past or earlier event adjacent to the present or later event. In both the known and questioned texts, the kind of disordered sequence I have referred to above occurred on a number of occasions, including such examples as 'the proof and evidence was given to the police', 'in the past years and months' and so on. In each case the sequence was disordered: thus, 'proof and evidence' defies the expectation that 'evidence' comes before 'proof': we have to collect the one to establish the other. Similarly, in 'the past years and months' we are in a disordered sequence because 'months' go to make up 'years'. The reader can verify this information using both internet (Google™) and corpus searches (e.g. BNC lists ['months and years': 30 – 'years and months': 1]).

Table 19.3. Internet frequencies of subject pronoun + past and present forms of to be

'I was and am'	155,000
'I am and was'	20,600
'he was and is'	174,000
'he is and was'	21,300
'she was and is'	55,100
'she is and was'	727
'we were and are'	50,300
'we are and were'	904
'they were and are'	122,000
'they are and were'	31,800

This kind of disordering also occurs at the syntactic level in the present case. Thus, we have a syntactic break caused by punctuation (a comma) in these examples:

- The police officer dealing with the case, stated that he did not believe me.
- . . . no proof of sexual activity having taken place, between Mary and myself.
- I and my partner, have over the past years and months, studied the case.

Here we have punctuation breaks occurring at syntactic boundaries, but not at boundaries where they are supposed to occur. Thus, in the first example the noun phrase 'The police officer dealing with the case' is separated from its complement, the verb phrase 'stated that . . .' by a comma. In the next example the verb phrase takes an indirect object 'between Mary and myself', yet the object, an intrinsic part of the verb phrase is separated from it. In the last example the noun phrase 'I and my partner' (itself a disordered sequence by convention) is connected to part of the verb phrase 'studied the case' by separating the auxiliary plus adverbial clause of time from the rest of the sentence in commas. Each of these three examples clearly illustrates how we can use syntactic punctuation as part of an analysis. A noted exponent of syntactic analysis is the American linguist, Carole Chaski.[3]

So far, therefore, in analysing these texts we seem to have found, at the (informal) semantic level, a disordering of sentence components, to do with tense and time, and other kinds of units, while at the syntactic level we have a syntactic break where we do not expect it. I suggest these two phenomena are really to do with ordering and arranging structures so that they either become disordered sequentially, or disordered structurally. They appear to be symptoms or indications of the same overall type. I suggest that this kind of disordering or re-arranging is something most of us do, but on a, typically, very small scale. What struck me about all of the texts in this inquiry was the scale and typology of the de-structuring. I then looked at the lexical level: here too something interesting appeared to be happening. A number of words were made into two words by the introduction of a space between them – for example, in both K and Q we find 'inter course' rather than 'intercourse':

KNOWN: At that interview the Police withdrew the charge of rape, and substituted it to one of unlawful sexual inter course.

QUESTIONED: Joe was again interviewed by the Police, the rape charge was dropped and changed to one of unlawful sexual inter course.

The break which occurs here is based on the notion that 'inter course' is two words. It is a disordering of the structure of the lexis. For the relevant meaning, the lexis does not store 'inter course' but 'intercourse'. The lexis probably stores, but for quite a different reason, a collection of prefixes in English, for example, 'inter' as in 'international', and of course it stores 'course'. Hence two storages – 'inter' and 'course' are possible, but not in the present context. What we essentially have, I am proposing, is a disorder of the structure of the lexis, seen in both K and Q, other examples of which include: 'photo copied', 'back fired', 'other wise' and 'some where'. As with the punctuation breaks in the sentence, we are seeing here a break – a word space – where one is not expected or licensed by the grammar.

There were also many spelling similarities across K and Q, for example, 'intensions', 'coarse' instead of 'course', a number of identical or near identical phrases, for example, 'for a so-called rape' *vs.* 'for the so-called rape', and so on. However, the spelling errors require a different kind of categorization than the other categories in terms of markedness and I will not be dealing with this topic here. The examples I have given here are simply a small sample of the similarities I found across the texts. In each case I prepare a 'match table' which lists how the known and questioned texts match each other with respect to a particular type of similarity. Here is an example shown in Table 19.4.

Table 19.4. Sample table of matches across known and unknown texts

Unknown	Matches	Known
is and has been [impotent]	**Temporal order**	*I am and was impotent*
	is and has been / am and was	
	Lexeme	
	impotent	
	Relevance	
	Both events in the past, yet the later (less temporally relevant) event is cited first	
Result: Match		Assessment: seems an unusual combination of common features

Some types of matches are more important than other types. Thus, exact matches of long clauses or whole sentences would have more value than, for example, misspelling matches. Document layout and style would have the least value, even less than orthographic (spelling, apostrophe, capitalization) matches. The point about matching characteristics is that each claimed match needs to be based on the concept of markedness, by which I mean a significant systematic difference from the norm. For example, if a candidate and the known author both spell 'receive' as 'recieve' this may indicate markedness, but it is not likely to be significant markedness. About 2 per cent of the population spell 'receive' incorrectly. It is not that unusual. When we look for markedness, we need to determine whether we are dealing with structures which are unusual or structures which are unconventional. These are two types of markedness.

With syntactic markedness we are on surer ground than studying features at a more superficial level, such as document layout: we know, as native speakers, that in English the form 'dog the' is marked because it violates a simple, easily observable, grammatical rule. Moving through the layers, with semantic or idiomatic markedness we are on less sure ground simply because these are not at the same layer of linguistic organization as syntactic structures (see Chaski 2001: 40). In the present case, it was my opinion that both known and questioned writers shared the same tendencies, namely, to disorder chronology, syntax and idiom. Problems or symptoms of very similar types pervade both sets of texts. The next question is calculating the similarities and differences. To do this, and following the work of the noted linguist Carole Chaski[3] I compute the number of marked constructions for each type of phenomenon, syntactic and otherwise. It is also important to list counter-examples. Recall, that it is not the linguist's task to *prove* anything. The task is one of discovery and demonstration, not *proof*.

How do forensic linguists judge their results? In the same way any other scientist does. If you have adequately tested your results and your method and you are able to quantify them statistically, you can repose a high level of confidence in them. I am using the word 'confidence' here in a non-technical sense. It is not the same thing as a statistical 'confidence level'. 'Confidence level' in statistics means the error rate you assign as the decision point for claiming an authorship match or, rather, a valid authorship comparison. One tool I use to assist in reaching a judgement is an order-of-importance table as shown in Table 19.5. This gives hierarchical order to markedness.

Table 19.5. Order-of-importance table of types of style features

Feature	No.	Comment	Assessment
Types of grammatical structure	1	See Chaski. A rare, unusual or erroneous structure across known and questioned. Knowledge of generative grammar helpful.	Significance depends on number and type of matches.
Punctuation	2	Unusual punctuation habits or punctuation errors can also be significant. Consider combining punctuation analysis with syntax.	Can be significant, but not necessarily on its own.
Idiom	3	Curious phrasing can be significant. Research its markedness wherever possible.	Depends on number and type of matches.
Spelling	4	Spelling errors, especially rare spelling errors. Look for dialectal spellings, such as US *vs.* UK spellings in English.	As above, but research degree of rarity.
Document layout	5	This can be of interest if the layout style is unusual. Beware, however, of cultural styles of layout.	Caution required, for example, US *vs.* UK *vs.* European styles.

Important notes: (i) when considering similarities and differences: avoid taking isolated instances of phenomena into account, (ii) consider the possibility of dialectal variation to account for (some) differences.

What this table says is that if we find two texts, supposedly independently produced, with a significant number of syntactic matches, then this is likely to be of greater significance than, say, matches relating to document layout. Finally, my last step is to apply a scale of judgements. Typically, linguists use a 10 point scale, though some linguists now favour using more complex statistical calculations, such as Bayesian likelihood ratios. At the end of the process the linguist offers an opinion as to whether there is a significant degree of similarity between two sets of text. In the present case I felt fairly certain of my conclusion and was able to assign an 8 out of 10 probability to my opinion. It is always better to be cautious. A scaled probability of 8 is quite high. It would be rare to apply a 9, and unheard of to apply a 10.

I handed in my report to the court and in due course the suspect was confronted with it. After about a month, the suspect appeared in front of the court continuing to deny the charge of rape but admitting to sexual assault. As I am sure the reader is aware, in order to protect the victim, I cannot be any more specific as to the details, but the work that was generated by applying forensic linguistic techniques to the evidence, I would hope, contributed in some small way to the result.

Notes

1. The British National Corpus, a large body of language of 100 million words, compiled by researchers at the University of Oxford.
2. Google, June 2007
3. Chaski, C. (1998). 'A Daubert-inspired assessment of current techniques for language-based author identification', US National Institute of Justice.

20

RETURN TO SENDER

In one of the western states in the United States of America, Fidesta McGreett consulted a family therapist on some personal matters. In the course of a session the therapist, Dr Pickwick, allegedly made certain comments of a suggestive nature to Ms McGreett and allegedly attempted physical contact with her. Following this visit, Ms McGreett made a complaint to the doctor's professional body. Several weeks after Ms McGreett made her complaint, the city where the McGreetts lived received an anonymous letter regarding her ability to care for her children, stating that Ms McGreett was suffering from 'premenstrual dysphoric disorder'. The city's Social Welfare Division was advised that as a result of this condition Ms McGreett was a danger to her children. The letter recommended careful monitoring of Ms McGreett's children for their own safety.

It is not easy to make positive attributions of authorship of anonymous letters, malicious or otherwise. The reason for the difficulty lies in the fact that malicious letters are generally short, and so contain relatively little textual data to evaluate or measure. Most malicious letter investigations I have undertaken concern the receipt of just one malicious communication, whereas in an ideal investigation the analyst would seek to have several questioned texts. I began asking myself what kind of specialist knowledge and experience of the topics discussed in the letter would the author of the letter need to have in order to write it, and what kind of knowledge would the writer need to have of the person who is the subject of the anonymous letter. There were four documents available for comparison: two letters sent by Dr Pickwick to his professional body, the anonymous letter sent to the City Social Welfare Division and a letter sent from Dr Pickwick's attorney to Dr Pickwick's professional body. In his first letter to the professional body, Dr Pickwick describes his method of working and gives a history of his development as a therapist. This is followed by an account of Ms McGreett's visit to his office. The second text is a further elucidation of Dr Pickwick's methods and beliefs regarding therapy, and further comments on Ms McGreett's visit. The third document is the anonymous letter. The last document is a letter

from Dr Pickwick's attorney, and is included because although there is
no question of its authorship being related to the present inquiry, it does
contain a rather singular phrase in the context of the present matter.

Forensic linguists sometimes carry out what is referred to as 'author
profiling'. This is not in any sense a psychological analysis or evaluation,
but an attempt at socially profiling the text's author, dealing with such
social variables as social status, age, gender, occupation, political or other
affiliation and level of education. Not all texts will provide clues to this
information. In fact, in many cases almost no personal data is revealed,
while on other occasions writers attempt to deceive the reader regarding
their social status, level of education and so on. Gathering social data
from malicious communications, therefore, needs to be done with care,
as should the interpretation of any such observations.

In the present instance, the writer of the anonymous letter begins by
informing the reader, the social welfare division, that Ms McGreett's
children may be in need of 'professional help'. The writer then goes on to
claim that Ms McGreett may be suffering from 'premenstrual dysphoric
disorder', that this disorder can lead to 'bouts of psychological instability', that it occurs in '7% of the female population', and that it is 'partly
hormonal and stress induced'. In the next paragraph the writer describes
the symptoms of the disorder, including anger, depression, a tendency to
suicidality and so on. The disorder's ill-effects are then further specified
as relating to tension and stress. The writer claims that Ms McGreett
has all these symptoms, and also that she suffers from bulimia, in addition to the dysphoric disorder. Finally, the writer urges social welfare staff
to 'take steps to monitor the well-being of the children, perhaps even
allocating them [sic] to a place of safety'. As we can see, the anonymous
letter is full of technical terminology relating to psychological matters.
The syndrome 'Premenstrual Dysphoric Disorder' is likely to be known
to relatively few people. The claim that it affects 7 per cent[1] of the 'female
population' is also likely to be somewhat specialist knowledge. The later
claim that Ms McGreett's bulimia causes her to resort to 'strange behaviors' also has an appearance of being authentic knowledge. Of particular
interest here is the word 'behaviors'. The word 'behaviors' is relatively
rare when compared with 'behavior', and its use among the general
public is likely to be very low. However, the use of the word 'strange'
in this context is somewhat populist, rather than specialist. The phrase
'psychological instability' is also somewhat populist – it is not the kind
of terminology that a psychiatrist, for example, might use. However,
despite these somewhat populist terms, the descriptions of the disorder,
its symptoms and its possible causes seemed to me to be somewhat beyond

the knowledge of the average person with regard to medical and psychological problems. The symptoms described and their possible or probable causes seem to be a description by someone who is familiar with the issues being discussed and purports to understand something of them. This is not remotely to imply that any credibility should be given to the claims made in the anonymous letter – on the contrary anonymous mail is rarely truthful, and this is particularly true when the intent of such letters is nothing other than character assassination, and therefore – under these circumstances, as with all malicious and hate mail communications – the descriptions, though perhaps correctly presented if referring to abstract states, are scarcely dispassionate. For the above reasons I concluded that the writer of the anonymous letter was likely to have some specialist knowledge of the issues discussed in it, especially with regard to psychological terminology.

Assuming for one moment that the entire contents of the anonymous letter were factually correct with regard to Ms McGreett, the question naturally springs to mind: 'what kind of person would know these things?' One assumes that most people do not broadcast vivid details of their physical or psychological ailments to the world, and – indeed – we have Dr Pickwick's own evidence that Ms McGreett was secretive in her behaviour, and that she specifically desired nobody to know the details of her symptoms. Apparently, according to Dr Pickwick, not even Ms McGreett's partner of more than 25 years knew much about her difficulties.

When we analyse the contents of Dr Pickwick's letters, Text 1 and Text 2, we note that many of the symptoms referred to in the anonymous text, apart from suicidality, and the violence of the mood swings is also mentioned in his own texts. In other words, it appears, from his own account, that Dr Pickwick is the sole person who is aware of the details of Ms McGreett's condition as it then allegedly was. Even the family doctor who recommended Ms McGreett to consult Dr Pickwick did not know that Ms McGreett was allegedly bulimic. Table 20.1 gives instances of the same, or nearly the same symptoms and circumstances being described across Dr Pickwick's own texts and the anonymous letters.

One perhaps slightly idiosyncratic point of interest is the use of the word 'homosexual' in the anonymous letter. Most of the references to Dr Pickwick's texts refer to his 'homosexuality', which he appears to give as his defence in having any sexual interest in Ms McGreett. In contemporary society 'homosexual' and 'homosexuality' are relatively rare when compared with 'gay' and 'gayness'. Internet searches suggest that 'gay' is about 15 times more common than 'homosexual'.[2] A second point concerns word composition. The anonymous letter uses the word 'maybe'

Table 20.1. Table of descriptions across the known and anonymous texts

Dr Pickwick's texts relating to Ms McGreett	The anonymous letter
'anger and depression'	Anger, Depression
'feel rejected'	'feelings of rejection'
'causing a lot of stress'	'a lot of stress' (specific reference to impending separation of Ms McGreett and husband)
'mood swings'	'Violent and unpredictable mood swings'
'bulimia behaviors'	'Bulimia . . . resorting to strange behaviors'
'they must never find out'; 'highly secretive'	'which she keeps hidden . . . to avoid detection'

Table 20.2. Results of internet searches of may be/maybe

'he maybe coming'	70
'he may be coming'	39,100
'she maybe coming'	40
'she may be coming'	978
'we maybe going'	214
'we may be going'	58,900

several times, where 'may be' is actually meant. I originally thought this phenomenon was not particularly rare, but then conducted the internet searches on Google (on 27 May 2008) as detailed in Table 20.2. This leads me to believe, that somewhere between 1/25 and 1/600 instances of the target string 'may be' are written as 'maybe'. This is rarer than I at first thought.

On this point it should be noted that neither Dr Pickwick, nor the writer of the anonymous note appear to be highly literate. Lack of high grade literacy among professionally qualified people is not as rare as one might think. I have a lawyer friend who always writes 'recieve' instead of 'receive', and 'perceive' as 'percieve'.

As we saw above, the anonymous note claims that Ms McGreett suffers from 'premenstrual dysphoric disorder' (PMDD). This is a highly specialized term normally reserved for psychiatrists and endocrinologists who deal in extreme premenstrual syndromes where behaviour is gravely affected. I seriously doubt whether even a highly qualified clinical psychologist would venture into making such a diagnosis, or even using such a term. Clinical psychologists will be aware that diagnosing such an illness would require the painstaking and dedicated efforts of a very experienced and senior psychiatrist. No psychiatrist would undertake such a task lightly. I also noted that Dr Pickwick did not mention this condition in his client notes.

Curiously enough, the letter from Dr Pickwick's attorney claims that Dr Pickwick suspects Ms McGreett suffers from precisely this condition, namely: 'It is our client's view that she may be suffering from a medical condition (viz. Premenstrual Dysphoric Disorder) that may be directly relevant to the credibility of the allegations she has made.'

The attorneys in question would, of course, not necessarily be familiar with the differences between psychological illnesses and illnesses which are reserved for the domain of medically qualified practitioners. I strongly suggest that Dr Pickwick has led his attorneys to believe that he understands the complexity of this condition sufficiently well to propose a possible diagnosis, even though from his notes on Ms McGreett's visit no questions were asked regarding regularity of menstruation, moods during the different phases of the menstrual cycle, how long she had allegedly been suffering from menstrual-related behavioural problems and so on. As the reader will appreciate, it is highly interesting that this medical phrase should occur in both the anonymous letter and in Dr Pickwick's texts. I suggest that not one person in 100,000 (other than properly qualified medical personnel or those with an interest in psychological and psychiatric symptoms) would even know this term. Literature searches on the internet suggest that the term 'premenstrual dysphoric disorder' is still controversial today, even though it was first used many years ago.

The term 'premenstrual dysphoric disorder' is described in the revised edition of the Diagnostic and Statistical Manual of Mental Disorders, known as *DSM-IV*.[3] Interestingly, Dr Pickwick himself refers to this publication, *DSM-IV*, in the context of 'histrionic personality'. The attorney's letter also seems to be suggesting that Ms McGreett's allegations have no credibility because of the possibility that she suffers from PMDD.

The attorney suggests that Ms McGreett should see a psychiatrist to determine if she has PMDD. If this suggestion came from Dr Pickwick then it further exposes his ignorance of what PMDD is and how it is to be diagnosed. As *DSM-IV* makes clear, the diagnostic process for PMDD is a lengthy one, and requires a high degree of self-monitoring of moods over a lengthy period during the luteal and follicular phases of the menstrual cycle. I take this detour into medical terminology in order to get across the difficulties of the diagnosis of PMDD. Against this, the attorney's letter appears, perhaps unwittingly, to echo the efforts of the anonymous letter to discredit Ms McGreett as a reliable, dependable, trustworthy person purely on the basis that she is suffering from an illness about which neither Dr Pickwick nor the attorney know very much. While it is of course forgivable that the attorney would be ignorant of these matters, it is scarcely conceivable that a therapist would claim to have diagnosed, or even comment on, a disease which very few psychiatrists would even *consider* beginning to attempt to diagnose without extensive consultation with a patient. Interestingly, the tactic of attempting to discredit female victims of sexual harassment or other attacks, is well known to include claims that the victim or alleged victim suffers from some form of premenstrual or other syndrome (see, for example, Raitt Zeedyk[4]). This attempt at discrediting Ms McGreett because of PMDD is something the attorney's letter and the anonymous letter both have in common. It is also interesting that there was no reference to premenstrual difficulties in Dr Pickwick's notes for the consultation with Ms McGreett. The above points aside, I noted that *both* the anonymous letter and the attorney's letter use the same formulation '. . . she may be suffering from' with reference to the alleged dysphoric disorder. This is illustrated in Table 20.3.

We may think that the phrase 'she may be suffering from . . .' is a common one, something we are sure to encounter almost every day, but in fact a search on the Google search engine reveals that this is not so. As a guide to the relative rarity of phrases, Coulthard and Johnson (2008: 198) describe a phrase which occurs on the same search engine 7,700 times as 'rare'.[5] Their phrase is 'I asked her if I could . . .' As an example of a phrase which is much rarer, there are only 169 instances of 'she may be suffering from . . .' at the time of writing (26 May 2008), making it

Table 20.3. Illustration of similarities in the two letters

Anonymous letter	she maybe suffering from	some form of	PMDD. (Premenstrual Dysphoric Disorder)
Attorney's letter	she may be suffering from	a medical condition (namely,	Premenstrual Dysphoric Disorder

Table 20.4. Internet frequencies of phrases

Phrase/string	Frequency
'she suffers from'	313,000
'she is suffering from'	133,000
'she could be suffering from'	4,500
'she seems to be suffering from'	1,180
'she appears to be suffering from'	427
'she may be suffering from'	169
Total	452,276

a very rare phrase. I append the relative frequencies of this and related phrases as found on Google in Table 20.4.

As can be seen from the above table, when compared to a number of phrases which include the formulation '"she" + [modal/auxiliary] + suffer/s/ing' the form 'she may be suffering from' is rarer by far than any of the others. If we calculate the frequency of 'she may be suffering from' as an overall percentage of the different formulations – and there are undoubtedly more possibilities – we end up with an infinitesmally small fraction, in this case 0.0004, which is four one-hundredths of 1 per cent. This undoubtedly makes 'she may be suffering from' a very rare phrase indeed.[6] On this basis, it seems to be beyond coincidence that the same, highly rare, phrase would occur in the anonymous letter as well as in Dr Pickwick's attorney's letter to the professional body.

I cannot be certain how this phrase entered the attorney's letter, but the most probable explanation is that the attorney noted down this phrase 'she may be suffering from . . .' (plus mention of the illness itself) as Dr Pickwick was saying it to him. It is inconceivable that the attorney could have got this information from anyone other than Dr Pickwick. Attorneys are not authors of client's texts in circumstances like these, but proxy authors. They write on behalf of a client. At the very least it is more probable that the author of this phrase was Dr Pickwick rather than the attorney. If we consider the other similarities between the anonymous text and Dr Pickwick's letters referred to above, the conclusion which appears to follow from the probable authorship of 'she may be suffering from', plus the specific reference to this rare disease, is that Dr Pickwick was also the most likely author of the anonymous text. Unfortunately, I was never able to verify this. Dr Pickwick's attorneys insisted that if their client had to attend a disciplinary hearing he ought to be able to question Ms McGreett in some detail regarding her health and her allegation against him. Knowing of her vulnerability as he certainly must have, this seemed to be an outrageous, perhaps even manipulative, demand by Dr Pickwick. However, it had the desired effect: Ms McGreett was unable to attend such a hearing and she was forced to drop her claim against the therapist.

Notes

1. Medical websites which discuss PMDD are not generally this specific, stating 'approximately 5%' or 'between "5 and 10%"', and so on.
2. Google on 27 May 2008: 'homosexual' = 21,000,000; 'gay' = 379,000,000

3. American Psychiatric Association, *Diagnostic and Statistical Manual of Mental Disorders (DSM IV)*, Fourth Edition, American Psychiatric Association, Washington, D.C., 1994.
4. Raitt F. R. and M. Suzanne (2000). *The Implicit Relation of Psychology and Law: Women and Syndrome Evidence*. London: Routledge.
5. Their example of a six-word string 'I asked her if I could' – which *seems* common enough – actually shows 7,770 instances on Google at the time their book was written (Coulthard and Johnson 2008: 197). Coulthard and Johnson describe this frequency (7,770) as 'rare'. Incidentally, the figure of 7,700 must have been observed several years ago – it is now 82,100. Note how much rarer 'she may be suffering from' is, at 169 occurrences.
6. On the other hand, it is important not to make the mistake of believing that only four one-hundredths of 1 per cent of the population would use this phrase. Common sense simply tells us that this is a very rare phrase.

21

WAS IT ERNIE OR RONNIE?

A conversation was being covertly recorded between a police officer and a suspect in a moving vehicle. One of the topics of conversation between the officer and the suspect was a third man, known as 'Ernie'. However, in one section of the tape a new name appeared to surface: 'Ronnie'. Police officers working on the case were not aware of anyone involved in the case by the name of Ronnie, and suspected that the name might be Ernie, but that the poor quality of the recording made it sound like Ronnie.

Disputed utterances can fall into one of two types. Either the utterance being disputed occurs only once and you have no way of comparing it with anything which is not disputed, or there are multiple instances of the utterance in undisputed form. The latter case is easier to deal with because you can then line up all your accepted instances on one side and compare them with all the instances of the disputed version. If there are no directly comparable exemplars you have to resort to other means, such as looking at the values of individual phonemes (speech sounds). When I was sent the tape I began by listening to it several times, and then recorded all the instances I could find where the name was undisputed. I excerpted each of these and obtained spectrogram values for the first phoneme, pronounced 'er'. The same procedure was followed for disputed instances of the name. The surveillance tapes in this case presented a number of acoustic problems including, in some instances, an intrusive electronic-sounding crackle, the sound of the car engine, the playing of the car radio, the movement of the target vehicle and so on. There were additional distracting noises, such as coughing, fidgeting and even playing with the radio dial. Both speakers had the habit of interrupting each other almost constantly, making it difficult to get continuous stretches of speech. The intrusive electronic noise I mentioned above had the annoying habit of sometimes coinciding with the first syllable of the disputed name, and this also complicated the acoustic analysis. It may be asked why as hearers we might confuse the name 'Ronnie' with the name 'Ernie'. Many people will, quite rightly, think that there are clear differences between these two names. For instance, one begins with a consonant and the other with a vowel. One has an 'er' sound and the other what we may think of as an 'o' sound. How can these names be compared with each other? While it is true that there are several major differences, there are also a number of similarities. Also, it is important to distinguish what we see on paper, that is, 'Ronnie' and 'Ernie' from what we actually hear. In our text-oriented society we take written forms so much for granted that language is now as much a visual experience as it is a speech and auditory one. This means that in highly literate societies we tend to listen less and look more. Regarding the similarities, first we notice that both names have two syllables. Secondly, the stress in each word is on the first syllable. Thirdly, both words have identical second syllables. Viewed this way we see that in reality the only differences are in the first syllable.

This may also be an opportunity to comment on the English vowel system. We are taught at school that English has five vowels a,e,i,o and u. What we are not taught is that this only applies to the writing system, and not to speech. What we have are not five vowels, but five vowel *symbols*. We do not have five vowels in English – the total is nearer to twenty depending on which dialect you speak. Think of all the different sounds you can produce which are represented by, or include, the letter 'a', one of the most overworked vowel symbols in the language: **all, at, aim, feat, fear, dialogue, quality, prepare, can** (when unstressed) and so on. It is part of the orthographic complexity which causes many hard-working teachers of English to want to tear their hair out. To simplify understanding of English vowels linguists have classified vowels on two axes of pronunciation. The vertical axis and the horizontal axis. On the vertical axis we can speak of a vowel as high, medium or low. On the horizontal axis the vowel is either back, mid or front. The first vowel in 'Peter', for instance, is a high, front vowel. For this vowel the tip of the tongue is at the top of the inside of the mouth and at the front of the mouth, not far behind the teeth. We can go through all the other vowels in the language and classify them in a similar way. For instance, the vowel in 'boot' is a low back vowel. The tongue is retracted and sits low in the mouth. To relate this to 'Ronnie', we see that the first vowel, 'o', is classified as an open back vowel. If you say 'Ronnie' and 'Ernie' or even just the first vowel in these names, you will see that the first vowel, written 'o' is not very far from the 'er' of 'Ernie' which is an open-mid central vowel. We can see this clearly from the vowel chart (courtesy of the International Phonetic Association) shown in Figure 21.1.

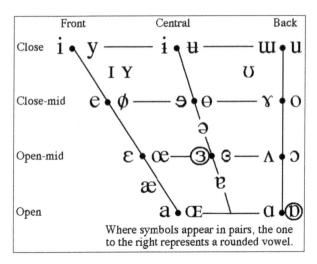

Figure 21.1. IPA Vowel chart, with target vowels circled (© IPA)

In Figure 21.1, the target vowels, the 'o' in 'Ronnie' (bottom right) and the 'er' in 'Ernie' have been circled. As can be seen the two vowels are not that far apart from each other on the vowel chart.

As listeners we are susceptible to influences from a number of sources. This can add to auditory confusion, including the difficulties of separating *signal* (what we want to listen to) from *noise* (everything we do not want to hear), the presence of co-articulation effects (i.e. the sounds surrounding the target sound), and subjective factors such as fatigue. Moreover, the speaker who appears to say 'Ronnie' when he is, I believe, saying 'Ernie' speaks a dialect of English in which the /r/ is not emphasized. When some speakers of English 'roll' the /r/ we refer to this as rhoticized 'r' or just *rhoticization*. In the male speaker's case in the present instance he speaks a dialect of English where the 'r' is not 'rolled'. Thus, there would sometimes not be a great deal of difference to the hearer, in rapid conversation, between 'Ernie', 'Ronnie' and even 'Rinnie' or 'Arnie'. In both 'Ernie' and 'Ronnie' the first vowel is in transition to, or moving to, the sound 'n', which is a further similarity between the two names. In the present instance I would argue that the initial phoneme of what sounds like 'Ronnie' is, in fact a vowel in transition rather than being /r/ itself. A further factor is that both 'r' and 'n' are articulated in the same part of the mouth, near to the area known as the alveolar ridge – above and behind the front teeth. All of these factors can contribute to auditory confusion between the two names.

However, I suggest that any auditory confusion is only applicable to people who might be listening to the conversation as outsiders. I do not think the participants themselves would have been confused. As 'overhearers' we are not aware of all the contextual factors relevant to the conversation, and, so – effectively – it would not normally be of any contextual importance to us whether the name was 'Ronnie' or 'Ernie'. However, the participants in the conversation were probably aware of the contextual factors, and so would have been able to make the necessary semantic distinctions at the time of the conversation. Thus, when the speaker referred to what sounded like 'Ronnie', the police officer he was speaking to did not comment on it or seek any information about it. Since the 'Ronnie' sounding name occurred two or three times in the space of just a few minutes, he had plenty of opportunity to do so. As speakers of a language, in this case English, we 'know' the rules of our language, including how to pronounce particular words. However, as humans we are subject to the limitations of performance, and so can easily mis-articulate words. All kinds of factors, including lack of concentration, age, fatigue, emotion and so on, might conspire to make this happen. It takes only fractionally different positions of the tongue, and perhaps very slight mistimings in our articulation to make a word like 'Ernie' appear to sound more like 'Ronnie'. When two speakers know each other well, and converse frequently – as was the case between the police officer and the suspect in question – it is not unusual for them to speak rapidly and pronounce their words with a certain degree of carelessness. It is symptomatic of their familiarity with each other.

At one point the male target says: '. . . put a bullet through Ernie's window'. The defence claimed that this was actually '. . . through Ronnie's window'. However, I was able to show that this confusion was brought about largely through the transition from the unstressed vowel in 'through' to the 'er' in 'Ernie'. Figure 21.2 shows a spectrogram of this, with the transcription in phonetic symbols below it.

What sounds like 'through Ron-' is in fact 'through Ern-', but, unusually, there is no stressed syllable in 'Ernie' and since there is no intervening consonant between the vowels the formants do not show much movement from the first to the second vowel. So, what we see is that the vowels in 'through' and 'er' are linked, again adding to any possible auditory confusion between 'Ronnie' and 'Ernie'.

In addition, I took a number of spectrogram measurements of the disputed and undisputed sections of the tapes. These showed that the

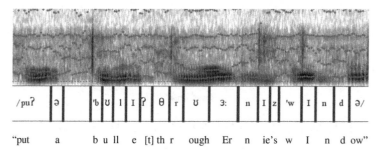

Figure 21.2. Spectrogram illustration of 'put a bullet through . . .'

formant measurements corresponded to an open-mid vowel rather than an open-back vowel. I also looked at how the speaker produced /r/ and found that this was quite definite on the spectrogram. I was therefore able to conclude that the disputed word was 'Ernie' than 'Ronnie'. The defence did not oppose this opinion and the suspect, Ernie, was convicted of conspiracy.

22

THE WITNESS STATED . . . BUT DID HE?

This case concerns the question of whether a young man witnessed a murder and whether the statement he gave to the police was admissible in court. Before telling you how this all came about I need to describe some aspects of Scottish law in connection with how statements may be obtained from witnesses. An important word to understand in this context is 'precognition', a term used exclusively in Scottish law. When parties to a case are drawing up the evidence they wish to present they are entitled to interview potential witnesses and take statements from them, whether or not these potential witnesses are reporting matters for or against the interest of their case. The process of taking statements from witnesses in this way is known as 'precognition', which loosely translated from Latin means something like 'knowing beforehand'. The point about precognosed statements is that they are confidential and may not be used in court. The reason that they cannot be used in court is that they are traditionally viewed as unreliable. However, there is another reason: precognition enables lawyers and police to get witnesses to give off the record, confidential statements about what they know or purport to know.

A ruling on the admissibility of precognosed statements was made by a judge, Lord Justice Clerk Thomson in 1958 in the case of Kerr vs. H.M. Advocate 1958 JC 14. In that case the judge said, with reference to the question of precognition: '. . . in a precognition you cannot be sure that you are getting what the potential witness has to say in a pure and undefiled form. It is filtered through the mind of another, whose job it is to put what he thinks the witness means into a form suitable for use in judicial proceedings. This process tends to colour the result. Precognoscers as a rule appear to be gifted with a measure of optimism which no amount of disillusionment can damp.' As can be seen, the judge in that case was concerned with the issue of reliability and impartiality. If a statement is questionable in these respects how can it be admitted in court? This was the issue in a recent murder case in Scotland.

The Glasgow[1] is a popular social club in the south of the city. It is a friendly drinking establishment which holds all kinds of family-oriented social events, especially at weekends. One evening a few years ago, a curry and karaoke night was in progress. It was well attended and club-goers were in party mood. At about 11.30 p.m. a number of people were involved in a dispute. Although nobody knew the cause of this dispute for certain, police thought it might have been related to a recent murder in the city and the shooting of a man at another city bar earlier. In the course of the dispute a man by the name of John McChesney, was stabbed. Staff immediately dialled 999 and the emergency services arrived. Many of the club-goers did not realize what had happened, as the Glasgow consists of several rooms. The karaoke had still been in full swing at the time of the stabbing. Mr McChesney was taken to a Glasgow Hospital where he later died. In the meantime, names and addresses were taken of everyone present, with a view to forming an interview list. The following day a Senior Investigating Officer was appointed, and an incident room was set up at a police station. A few days later Jimmy McBurt, aged 19, gave a statement to police officers. McBurt said he had been to the toilet at the club in the course of the evening, that he had been there for only a few minutes, that nobody else was there at the time and that after that uneventful event he returned to where his friends were sitting in the club. He said he had not realized anything had happened until the police arrived. In the meantime, the murder inquiry was ongoing and a man called Harry Edinburgh was arrested and charged. At the same time police officers were liaising with family members of the deceased. On one occasion they met with McChesney's brother, Howard, who told them that Peter McChesney, his nephew, had met with Jimmy McBurt, who was a friend of his, for a drink, and that in the course of that conversation McBurt had told his nephew, Peter McChesney, that he had in fact observed Harry Edinburgh entering the toilet with a knife and had then washed blood from it. According to Peter McChesney, McBurt had said that a man called Brian James had held the door closed at the time to prevent people seeing Edinburgh with the knife.

With this information in mind Jimmy McBurt was re-interviewed by the police. The main idea of this second interview was to fill in the gaps from the first interview. The detectives interviewing Jimmy McBurt noted that he had learning difficulties. He seemed very young for his age. In addition, he had a drink problem. McBurt was unaware of the fact that Harry Edinburgh had already been arrested on suspicion of murder. In most of the United Kingdom, interviews are usually recorded on audio cassette tape. In Scotland it is not usual for witnesses to be recorded, and I do not have any information as to whether Jimmy McBurt was cautioned with regard to the truth of his statement. At this stage of the inquiry he probably was not, as he was still being seen as a witness.

The detectives told McBurt that he was being re-interviewed because they had new information, namely, that McBurt had told John McChesney's son that he had seen Edinburgh in the club toilet washing a knife. The form of the interview is not in dispute. Officers asked questions, McBurt responded, and officers then told McBurt what they would write down. It is reported by the officers that he did not disagree with the version put to him. In this way a statement was compiled and Jimmy McBurt signed it. McBurt was evidently a reluctant witness. The officers agree they had to press him somewhat in order to get his story, although there is no suggestion of oppressive interviewing. According to the statement, McBurt eventually admitted he had seen Edinburgh with the knife and Brian James at the door preventing anyone else from coming in. At the end of the interview the statement was read to McBurt and he was asked if he wanted to alter anything. He did not say he wanted to. When asked why he had not given this information earlier, McBurt said that he was scared of Harry Edinburgh.

At his trial, McBurt's advocate made a motion for McBurt's statements not to be admitted into evidence. The advocate pointed out that the two statements had been taken in completely different ways. Whereas the first statement was almost a verbatim account, the second statement had been compiled from questions and answers. The question, therefore, boiled down to one of who the author of that statement really was. It was impossible, the advocate said, to determine how much had been Jimmy McBurt's own input, and how much was the officers' input. Clearly, in the opinion of the advocate, the police had entered the interview with a preconception as to Edinburgh's guilt. They could not, therefore, be objective in the taking of the statement. Manifestly, the young man had been precognosed. Therefore, in the absence of any admissible statement there was no evidence to be brought against him. While there was no requirement for a statement to be in the precise words of the witness, it was still necessary that, for any statement to be admissible in court, it had to have been taken impartially. In the present case, the advocate argued, this had not happened: the police gave McBurt their interpretation of events and even though he had apparently agreed with them this was irrelevant. The judge agreed and the case was dismissed.

The Crown appealed, largely on the grounds that the judge had misinterpreted the law: the admissibility of evidence was no longer related to whether it had been given under conditions of precognition. They cited Thompson *vs.* Crowe, per Lord Justice General Rodger at pages 192 and

202, who stated that, providing the facts of the case have been established, questions of admissibility of evidence were questions of law for the judge. In other words, it was up to the judge as to whether the precognition issue was to be of any significance or not. At a preliminary hearing convened to decide whether the Crown's appeal should be allowed, the discussion centred on questions relating to the definition of precognition, exceptions to the inadmissibility of precognosed statements, and the thorny question of how to define a statement. Theoretically, a statement can be any utterance by a witness or suspect on a matter relating to an offence. However, as early as the 1850s, judges had routinely discounted precognosed statements as admissible in evidence. In a bankruptcy hearing in the 1860s (Emslie *vs.* Alexander) the issue was whether what a bankrupt had said at an earlier judicial examination was admissible. This is the earliest precedent for courts being able to reject precognosed statements. The judge in Jimmy McBurt's original trial cited this point. However, the point at issue for the appeal judges was not so much related to the question of the admissibility of precognosed statements, but the much more basic one of what constituted a precognosed statement and, even more fundamentally, how to define the term 'statement'.

The judges found that there are three basic types of statement: one obtained from potential witnesses on behalf of a party to a case; one obtained by police when investigating a case and one taken under oath at an *ex parte* hearing (i.e. without the requirement of parties to attend a hearing). The first type, statements obtained on behalf of parties to a case, are precognitions and are not usually admitted. In the second case, police officers are required to gather evidence to investigate a crime. They usually do so under authority from the procurator fiscal (the prosecutor) or from a senior police officer. It would severely hamper any criminal investigation if such statements fell under the precognition rule. Manifestly, according to the appeal judges, a police statement could not be classified in this way. The defence's argument, that the police investigation was already underway, and that therefore the statement must be a precognition, was not accepted by the appeal judges. The judges then addressed the issue of the structure of Jimmy McBurt's statement. It was clearly in narrative form, as though it had been told by McBurt as a story. However, everybody knew, and admitted, that it had come about as a series of questions and answers. Was this a reason to exclude it as admissible evidence? Although a process of translation is involved in converting the events from a question and answer format to a narrative, this does not automatically invalidate the resulting statement, providing that the process of obtaining the statement is fair to the witness (or defendant).

The judges, therefore, ruled that the appeal could go ahead, meaning that Jimmy McBurt could be tried for perjury. In my report I argued that the problem was not the second statement, but the first. I could not understand why McBurt said in his statement that when he had been to the toilet there was nobody else there and that nobody had been by the door trying to get in or out. Why would police have asked this? Why would McBurt have volunteered it? Negative assertions which purport to be spontaneous are necessarily suspect: they tell about something that is not. This is completely unnatural unless there is good reason for it. I argued that the police must have asked him these questions, but I did not understand why, unless they already had information about him going to the toilet. I also argued that there had to be serious doubts about McBurt's ability to understand the issues. I based this on an interview I had with him. I began by asking him:

Q: Jimmy, would you just give us a little bit of information about yourself, tell us your date of birth where you were born . . . your age . . . stuff like that.

A: Born Glasgow, date of birth's fifth of the fourth 1985, currently staying at Govan, it's just a temporary house I'm maybe getting another one tomorrow.

One of the things I had asked him was his age. Note that in his reply he does not mention his age. There were other instances of the same kind of partial attentiveness to questions. Asked what he had been doing on the day of Mr McChesney's death – a day that had apparently changed his life forever, he replied without hesitation that he had been out drinking with friends during the day, but when asked to name them was unable to do so, although they are mentioned in his statement. Asked whether he had met other friends when he had seen Mr McChesney on that particular day he was unable to name the pub where this had happened though he could describe it in some detail. However, it was a generic description, and included items such as 'pool table', 'bar' and so on. This seemed to be the kind of pub he always went to and so I doubted if it was an actual recollection. It was probably more likely a general recollection about drinking establishments. I wondered if his ability to process written language was any better than his ability to process speech.

I now took a document I had prepared earlier. It purported to be a waiver allowing me to interview him and tape-record the interview. This is an issue in the present case because McBurt signed each page of his police statement. Most people would infer from these signatures that he was fully aware of what he was signing when he signed it. I had therefore devised an authorization letter, which he would sign, allowing me to interview him and tape-record the interview. There were two copies of the letter. The first copy was phrased as follows:

Glasgow, Wednesday, 23 May 2007

My name is Jimmy McBurt. I hereby grant permission for my voice to be recorded and the recording to be used in any appropriate way for my court case.

However, the second copy was a deliberately misspelled, nonsensical version of the first copy and was phrased as follows:

Glashgow, Weddingsday, 23 May 2007

My namne is Jimmy MoBurt. I hereby can't permission for my vote to be recorded and the re-coding to be misused in any inappropriate way for my count cage.

I asked Jimmy to look at both of these and to sign them if he agreed with what they said. I watched him as he took his time studying the documents. I asked him if they said the same thing. He held them side by side, and nodded his head. Then he signed them. This was all with the agreement, and in full view of, his legal representative, who also witnessed his signatures. Jimmy McBurt did not observe any of the errors in the copy, even though it misspelled his name as 'MoBurt', 'Glasgow' as 'Glashgow' and allowed me – effectively – to 'misuse' the tape-recording of his voice in any 'inappropriate' way I saw fit. I felt bad about putting him through this, but I felt these issues related directly to his ability to process written language. The documents were as simple as I could make them given the information they needed to contain. As a result of this test it was clear to me that if McBurt was having difficulty understanding a simple two-sentence document, he would certainly not be able to process a ten-page statement.

Therefore, contrary to the view of the appeal judges, I believed that the authorship of the statements was an issue. I suggest that somebody who is incapable of processing relatively simple questions put to them, or is unable to observe basic errors in written language cannot be held accountable for the authorship of language produced in concert with others. I am not suggesting any bad faith on the part of the police officers concerned. On the contrary, there is evidence that they were entirely sympathetic to Jimmy McBurt's difficulties and made every attempt to help him. However, I believe that they underestimated the difficulties he would have had in rejecting ideas put to him which he did not agree with, and that they overestimated his ability to comprehend and connect events. In court, McBurt appeared to be able to give answers to the questions he was asked by the prosecution, but the discourse of the courtroom is completely different from the discourse of the police station, particularly with the way in which questions are asked and answered. If there is one skill lawyers have above the rest of us it is to build a narrative from deceptively simple questions, beginning with the most fundamental. They assume absolutely nil knowledge, and they move at a snail's pace through a series of questions, building the witness's story one brick at a time. They never ask two questions together, always one question at a time, pausing before going onto the next question. Every point is carefully broken down to its elements. Police officers used to interviewing can do this too, but there is an important difference. The police officer's question is open-ended. It can have almost any answer. In fact, if the interview is to be fair, then the questions must be open-ended. The lawyer's question is not designed in this way: it usually has only one of two answers, yes or no. Equivocation is not possible. The answer to any other type of question is almost always known by the lawyer in advance, and its answer is always a single time, a single place, a single person, a single action. Again, the narrative is built with absolute adherence to the one brick at a time rule. For this reason, I suggest that McBurt's performance on the witness stand was not a surprise. The issues were very clear. Had he gone to a club that evening? Yes. Which one was it? The Glasgow. Did he go there with anyone else? Yes. Who? His friend's grandfather. Had he had anything to drink? Yes. Had he seen Mr McChesney? Yes. Had the police come? Yes. Had they interviewed everybody? Yes.

I suggest the important questions are not so much whether Jimmy McBurt told the truth. In cases where an individual is incapable of understanding a complex narrative and cannot be the sole author of that narrative, then truth becomes an authorship issue. This is because if that person is not solely or wholly responsible for a statement's content, then neither can that person be totally responsible for its veracity. What was recorded at that interview may well be true, but McBurt was not the sole author of that truth. Therefore, when he was on the witness stand and he was asked to defend what he had said at the police station he could not do so. The examples I have given above of his written and spoken responses clearly demonstrate an inability to understand and articulate complex issues, an inability to concentrate on sequences of events, and an inability to connect abstract concepts. I suggest the statement he gave should have been excluded on this simple basis – that he was not the sole, or perhaps even most significant author of that statement.

The judges found differently. Jimmy McBurt is currently serving a 3-year sentence for perjury.

Note

1. All place and people names changed.

23

PEOPLE TRAFFICKING AND THE LANGUAGE OF TRAUMA

The fall of the Iron Curtain and the expansion of the European Union has meant an opening up of the countries of eastern Europe to the west and has resulted in greater freedom and mobility for millions of people. Unfortunately, it has also meant an increase in criminal activity originating in some eastern European countries, especially in the areas of drug smuggling and people trafficking. Over the years I have been involved in a number of such cases. To protect the innocent I will need to change names, places and other details. I am also condensing a number of cases into the stories of just two of the women involved in order to further reduce the possibility of identification.

In the east European country of Karasta,[1] unemployment among the young is very high, as it is has traditionally been in several parts of eastern Europe. This has laid young people open to all kinds of abuse from unscrupulous gangs determined to profit from the misery of others. A particularly vicious form of profiteering is to be had if you are prepared to sell other people into prostitution. In 1999, a young woman from Ivdov, the capital city of Karasta, was robbed by neighbours. When she complained to the police they violently ejected her from the police station, telling her that she was wasting their time. 'If you ever want a man for the night' one of the policemen told her, 'just call me'. A few days later she was beaten up and mugged. She had a 3-year-old son to support, her husband having walked out on her the previous year in pursuit of another woman. Soon, however, her luck seemed to change. On the way home from her factory job one day, a car stopped and the driver, a pleasant young man in his mid-twenties named Roman, offered her a lift. Katerina was pleased to accept and it soon became an established thing that he was somehow outside her place of work almost every day to drive her home. In turn, she cooked for him, washed his clothes and the two soon became friends though the relationship did not go any further. One day Roman offered her a job. He told her it wasn't in Karasta, but in England. Some good friends of his, he said, were looking for a housekeeper. They lived in the country where they had a large estate. The husband was elderly and, as much as anything else, the wife needed company. She would have her own apartment in the house, her own car to do shopping in, could invite friends over from time to time and eventually, if all went well, her little boy could join her. It sounded idyllic.

Katerina asked Roman what she would have to do to secure such a position, thinking that there might be a catch in it. All she would have to do, he said, was to get ready to go to England. He would arrange the whole trip. He needed a photograph of her to send to the couple. He would pay her fare and what he called 'arrangement' fees, but aside from that her money would be her own. She would have to pay him back but it wasn't much. In any case, she could earn far more in England as a housekeeper than working in a factory in Karasta. She agreed. At the same time Roman asked her to speak to one of her friends at the factory because he was looking for a waitress for a top quality restaurant in London. She agreed and soon recruited a younger colleague, Maria. In the meantime she also persuaded her mother to look after her son while she worked abroad. Soon Katerina and Maria obtained their passports and were on their way to England. They both thought it strange that just before they got to the German border they were bundled into the back of a truck with what seemed to be several tons of fruits and vegetables and were told not to talk, but since this seemed to be the only way to secure a good future for herself and her son, she accepted it. There were several other young women on the trip with Katerina and Maria, and the group soon found themselves in France. At Calais they were given new passports with different names in them. Their own passports were taken away. The passports they were given were obviously false, but what was more alarming was that the passports were not even of their own country.

It was useless to protest, however, because – for the first time – they were informed that they each owed the 'organizer' thousands of pounds for arranging their trip. They were told to memorize their passport details and to be 'convincing' in the event of being questioned. The entire operation, from the time they left Karasta, seemed highly organized. A number of men, including Germans, French, Dutch and Belgians had been involved. Arriving in the United Kingdom posed no problems. Officials barely looked at their passports before stamping them and processing them through customs. On the other side they were met by a friendly couple who drove them to a northern city. It was late at night before they reached their destination. They were divided into pairs and each pair was taken to a flat. A protest from Katerina that this was not the job she had been offered almost resulted in her being assaulted.

Maria, who barely understood that this northern city was not London as she had been promised, intervened and restored order. They had hardly had time to unpack before their 'boss' arrived. Immediately the girls felt afraid of him. He told them to sit down because he had some news for them. 'This is where you will live' he said, indicating the apart-ment with its one bedroom. 'Every day I will send men to see you. You will do what they want. If you leave the house you must phone me first because if I come here and you are not here I will fine you £50. Every week you must pay me £200 towards your debt and half of what you earn. After that your money is yours'. Slowly, it sunk into the girls' con-sciousness that they were to be prostitutes. 'Do not refuse' the 'boss' told them, 'or it will go badly for you'. He paused: 'We did have a refusal from one woman' he said threateningly, 'but I don't know where she is now. I believe she is not happy'.

He must have read Katerina's mind because he then said: 'Do not think of going to the police. In England the police are very strict. They will first put you in jail for five years and then send you home. Everybody will know you have been a prostitute'. He lit a cigarette. 'I will let you go home when you have paid your debt and made me enough money. It has been very troublesome getting you here. Do not disappoint me. Do everything the gentlemen tell you to do. If you are very good I might give you one day off every month, but if you give me a hard time I will fine you and you will have no time off. Co-operate and be happy'.

After the boss left, the women were in a state of shock, not knowing what to do. The situation seemed hopeless. They knew nothing about England and could not imagine that the police would be sympathetic to their plight. The threat of prison in a foreign country terrified them. They decided they had to do as they were told. Early the next morning one of the boss's many messengers arrived with two mobile phones. This was the boss's preferred method of contacting them to tell them when a new 'client' was on the way. There were not many days when the mobile phones did not ring. The clients were a bewildering array of men of all ages who expected the girls to cater to their every whim, including bond-age, caning and whipping. It seemed there was nothing they were not expected to put up with, no limits to the abuse the boss had in store for them. Every Friday he would arrive to collect the rent, an instalment on the debt and his 50 per cent of their earnings. It did not leave them much over, however hard they worked. Some of their clients were also informants of his and reported back how much they paid for the services.

Hence, it was impossible to lie about how much they were paid. Prices were fixed anyway. They were not allowed to keep any tips they were given. For a gruelling 9 months they did the boss's every bidding, frightened to go out, frightened to talk to strangers, too terrified to complain. Finally, the day came when the boss told them they could go back home. They had paid their debt, he said, and in any case they were looking, as he described it 'old'. 'Nobody wants to sleep with you anymore' he told them, 'you are past your best'. Despite the intended insult it was the happiest day of their lives. They flew back to Karasta the next day.

Back home the women decided to complain to the police, hoping they would arrest Roman, their procurer. But this was more easily said than done. Outwardly friendly and sympathetic, the police did nothing to apprehend Roman. One day a policeman visited Katerina at her home and told her that Roman had 'powerful' friends and they could do nothing. A while later Katerina received a phone call from Maria telling her to watch out: she, Maria, had been badly beaten up by someone warning her to stay away from the police. That next day two men forced their way into Katerina's apartment and beat her up in front of her child. For several days she kept getting phone calls in which an unknown voice told her that she had better 'shut up'. Terrified, she went to her mother's house in the hope of remaining out of sight. Not long afterwards Maria turned up, saying that it was unsafe for them to remain in Karasta. After some discussion, they decided to return to the United Kingdom and seek asylum. In fear for their lives they managed to get out of the country and take a flight to London. At the port of entry they gave a statement about their reasons for seeking asylum. They were admitted into the United Kingdom, with the understanding that their case would be investigated.

This was where I got involved. I was asked by the agency dealing with their case to compare what the women had told the immigration officers about the reason for their first trip to the United Kingdom with what they had told the police in their own country when they had returned there after leaving England. One thing that concerned the agency about the women's statements was that they did not seem to convey any emotion. Their view was that if the women had been forced into prostitution they would have reacted against it, and would have expressed their feelings in their statements. At first sight there seemed to be some truth in this. For example, describing her entry into the United Kingdom Katerina had said:

We were transported in a ship to England. We arrived at night time. An official stamped my passport and I walked through customs.

I met a man and a woman there. They drove me to the city of –. There I was assigned an apartment with my friend. After a time the employer arrived and told me my duties. He told us we had to repay our debts to him and therefore we must function as prostitutes as there was no other work. We decided to follow his instructions.

I had to agree with the immigration agency. This account did seem to be lacking in expression or emotion. I wondered if perhaps it was the translation process which was at fault. Had the work perhaps been done by someone more used to translating official government documents than everyday human narratives? I decided to commission a second translation. This time I was able to choose the translator myself, and so I chose an English graduate who had worked in Karasta for several years and who actually had a degree in the language. To my surprise, however, there was little difference in tone from the earlier translation:

We travelled by ferry to England, arriving at night. My passport was stamped by an official and I passed through customs. Outside I met a couple who drove me to the city of –. Maria and I were allocated an apartment. Soon our employer arrived and told us what we would have to do. He said that we had a debt to repay, and that we must work as prostitutes as there was no other employment available. We decided to obey him.

Looking at other sections of the statements, I found them similarly expressionless. For instance, speaking about the job she had been offered while still in Karasta, Katerina had said in her statement to the police in her own country:

Roman told me I would have a good life in England. The job was to be as a housekeeper at a country house. He said it was a very nice job. He said I would soon earn enough to bring my son to England. My son would have a better education than at home in Karasta. I did not know I was going to be a prostitute. They told Maria she was going to be a waitress. They said it was at an expensive restaurant in London.

This differed little from the account which Katerina gave to UK officials:

There was no talk of prostitution and it is something I would never have agreed to. Roman told me there was a good job at someone's house. He said I was going to be the housekeeper there and the salary was good. I could eventually be allowed to have my little boy to live with me and he would attend school in England.

There were two matters the agency dealing with Katerina's claim for asylum had to resolve. The first issue, which did not directly involve linguistics, was whether the women were really under threat from violence or even death if they went back to Karasta. The second question was whether the account given to immigration officials in the United Kingdom was at variance with the account given to the police back in Karasta.

The question of veracity in language is not strictly a linguistic matter, but the structuring of personal narrative and discourse is. Thus, Martin and Rose (2003: 22-23),[2] discourse analysts working in the tradition of M. A. K. Halliday, have analysed how people form their attitudes, either to positive or negative experiences. They see a central outcome to personal narrative as being what individuals learn from an experience. This is then structured into an appraisal and evaluation system. According to Martin and Rose we form our attitudes from our evaluations and appraisals and we use language to negotiate those attitudes. An important component in all these structures is how we feel and then how we express those feelings. I will shortly report on what Martin and Rose had to say on the linguistic expression of feeling in people's personal life stories and why I believe this did not apply in the present case. As I mentioned above, what interested me about the women's narratives was that they seemed almost devoid of expressions of feeling. This may have been why the immigration agency felt that their accounts might be unreliable. Given that many asylum seekers will have left their home countries under traumatic conditions I wondered whether anybody had specifically researched the ways in which emotion is expressed in asylum and immigration statements.

There has a been a shift in the terminology applied to people fleeing their country of birth or residence in recent years, and in place of the term 'refugee' we now have the more clinical 'asylum seeker'. The term 'refugee' seems to imply that it is an understood thing that someone in danger will flee from it. Nowadays, 'refugees' have been largely replaced, in Europe at least, by 'asylum seekers'. The victim is thus no longer *fleeing*, but *seeking*. It seems to me, purely from a linguistic point of view, that the onus is now on asylum seekers and migrants to prove that they should be granted the status of refugee, of someone who has valid reasons for fleeing from persecution. More often than not, such people have to go through the process of proving their case at the very time when they are experiencing the most trauma. John Wilson and

Boris Drozdek[3] are pioneers in the area of assessing trauma among refugees, victims of war and other asylum seekers. They point out that

> [A]sylum seekers, refugees, and war and torture victims have been cast adrift on the seas of fate ... people who have been uprooted from their homelands and thrust into the very uncertain world of seeking shelter ... as victims of war, political upheaval, or catastrophe, they journey from a home base of known certainties to unknown places in an unfamiliar culture. (Wilson and Drozdek 2004: 3)

According to Wilson and Drozdek the whole process of becoming a refugee and then seeking asylum in another country is, in the modern world, a humiliating and traumatic experience for many. Not the least traumatic part of what they undergo is proving their need for asylum in the first place. This whole process often produces what the authors term 'broken spirits', people who have lost not just their home and their roots, but also their entire culture, contact with their families, but also – from the linguistic point of view – their language in its natural environment. Explaining what has happened to you to an official in a neon-lit room at dawn while sipping coffee out of a plastic cup is never going to be easy, but doing it through an interpreter who may not have time to be sympathetic to you might very well make matters worse.

One point that occurred to me early on was that we should not judge the statements of these women by reference to our own cultural values. We are perhaps mistaken in our expectation that they would speak of very personal feelings and reactions openly to officials such as police and immigration officers. Even within their own culture it may be very difficult to speak of such matters. I noted from the documentation that the police and immigration officials to whom they had given their statements were all men, both in Karasta and in the United Kingdom. This may have made matters worse. Not only did these young women have to open up to strangers, but these strangers were men, probably old enough to be their fathers. How to discuss intimate matters with such people – in a language which meant nothing to the person you were talking to? We tend to think of language as just a 'system of communication', but it is much more than that. Language is part of our phatic system – our emotions, moods and reactions – as much as it is part of our cognitive system. When we speak it is not just our thoughts we are expressing but our feelings as well. But if we cannot express our feelings – owing to the trauma we are experiencing, then it is hardly surprising if our thoughts, too, are blocked. It is interesting that since the publication of DSM-IV[4] trauma is now defined in terms of its effect on the victim, rather than as an 'object-ive event'.[5] What this means is that the victim's appraisal of trauma now takes centre stage in psychological and other assessments, rather than society, politicians or bodies of 'experts' defining what trauma is.

Well known linguistic and social effects of trauma are that the victim shows signs of being withdrawn, is silent for extended periods, is unable to articulate and difficult to engage with ('dissociated').[6] I could not be certain, but reading the statements of these abused women, it seemed to me inevitable that the language found in them would be flat and almost non-descript. Even if they shared our culture's aspirations on the desir-ability of expressing what they felt, and wanted to do so (albeit through an interpreter to an unknown official of the opposite gender), the trauma of their experiences was likely to have a severely dampening effect on anything they said.

Earlier, I referred to the research of Martin and Rose regarding the role of emotion in the language of personal life stories. Martin and Rose structure their book around the narrative of a young woman who grew up in apartheid South Africa. She gives her life story, beginning with life under the Nationalist government before 1994. She describes many traumatic events. I was struck by the language she used to describe what she saw and felt and the contrast with the women from eastern Europe who had been trafficked into prostitution. Here is an example where the young South African woman describes some of the abuse she went through after being arrested:

> 'On arriving . . . at [the] police station . . . I was screamed at, verbally abused . . . slapped around . . . punched . . . I was told to shut up . . . I was questioned . . . told that I was lying . . . smacked again and . . . knocked down.' Describing her reaction to what happened to her the young woman wrote: 'I can't explain the pain and bitterness in me . . . I was torn to pieces.' (Martin and Rose 2003: 72–75)

What we notice about this language is how graphic it is. Even though the writer says she is unable to 'explain the pain and bitterness' we nevertheless get a very good sense of it from her descriptions (to which I have not had space here to do justice). I wondered why there was such a difference between the way this woman used language to describe her experiences and the language of the women who had been trafficked.

First, I would say, we cannot underestimate the effect that trans-lating something has. This woman is writing in her own language,

English. She is able to be very precise, to evaluate the effect of her words and, if she finds them unsatisfactory, to use other ones. The Karastan women were unable to do this. They were having to rely on someone else to act as the vehicle for their experiences. Secondly, the South African woman was writing at a time when the trauma she had experienced had long since ceased to be a daily reality. She had, to some extent, emerged from her sufferings and had undergone considerable healing in the meantime. In linguistic terms she had successfully *negotiated* her trauma. Moreover, she had written her account in a spirit of reconciliation within the framework of the national reconciliation her country was undergoing at the time. On the other hand, the Karastan women had had to describe their experiences soon after experiencing them. They had had no opportunity to come to terms with them. They were still living the various traumas of having been tricked into prostitution, of having suffered physical and verbal abuse at the hands of their tormentors, of then having returned home and being assaulted, and of subsequently having had to flee their home country and seek refuge in a country where they had not had pleasant experiences, but which was the only other country they knew, apart from their own. They had had to tell their story through the medium of another language to strangers while still suffering the effects of these traumas. Thus, I suggest we should be very careful when evaluating the life stories of others, whether in the form of evidence in court, statements to police and other officials or accounts read in newspapers. We tend to equate real life stories with what we may have read in books or heard about in the media, but not all stories of suffering and degradation are the same, and unlike fiction many do not have happy endings. Above all, different cultures approach such experiences in vastly different ways.

I reported these observations to the agency handling their case, with the caveat that my opinion was moving dangerously close to psychological and ethnological issues rather than purely linguistic ones, and that the agency should consider getting further advice on these matters from forensically qualified people in those fields. At the beginning of this chapter I mentioned that I would be condensing the trafficking experiences of a number of women into the stories of just two of them. Most of the cases I have condensed into this chapter have been going through the asylum system for a number of years now. Some of these women are still waiting to hear if they will have to return to their home countries. Even with the best will in the world, the wheels of asylum justice move with painful slowness. The trauma of these women is not over.

Notes

1. Obviously an invented name. The language of this mythical country I will call 'Karastan', as also its people. The capital 'Ivdov' is also an invented place name.
2. Martin J. R. and D. Rose (2003). *Working with Discourse*. London: Continuum.
3. Wilson J. and B. Drozdek (2004). *Broken Spirits: The Treatment of Traumatized Asylum Seekers, Refugees, War and Torture Victims*. London: Routledge.
4. *DSM-IV: The Diagnostic and Statistical Manual of Mental Disorders* (DSM), published by the American Psychiatric Association, 1994.
5. A. Brunet, V. Akerib and P. Birmes (2007). 'Don't Throw Out the Baby With the Bathwater (Post Traumatic Stress Disorder Is Not Overdiagnosed)'. *Can J Psychiatry* (52) 501–502. These authors note that post traumatic stress disorder is routinely underdiagnosed and underestimated in society in general.
6. Rick Curnow, in a public lecture on 'Trauma: a psychoanalytic perspective'. Adelaide, 2007. Found at: http://www.aipsych.org.au/articles/aip_trauma_psychoanalytical.pdf on 24 May 2008.

GLOSSARY

Acquired property: A property or faculty that humans acquire through social interaction, as opposed to an inherited property. Language is considered to be an acquired property. See also 'Inherited properties'.

Advocacy: The process whereby an expert witness will *de facto* act for the prosecution or defence. The practice of advocacy by expert witnesses is highly unethical and can lead to an expert witness's disqualification in a trial. See also 'Impartiality'.

Authorship: The process whereby language is produced by an individual writer or speaker, or by a group of writers or speakers.

Authorship attribution: The activity of attempting to assign a particular text to one or more candidate authors (see 'Authorship'). It is perhaps obvious to state – but nevertheless important to emphasize – that authorship attribution (or identification) is not document examination or handwriting analysis, but the analysis of the structures of the language.

Average: See 'Mean'.

Bully mail: A communication, usually by means of a mobile phone text, designed to intimidate its recipient. A practice which has been noticed with increasing frequency, especially among young people of school and university age.

Candidate author: A candidate author is an author whose texts are being compared to a suspect or questioned text. In an inquiry there is usually, but not inevitably, more than one candidate author.

Collocation: The occurrence of two words in close proximity to each other. See, for example, the chapter 'A case of medical disinformation' where 'informaton' is described as a regular collocate of 'disclose'.

Computational linguistics: The study of the properties of language by computational means, using calculations and statistics. Hence the description *computational linguist*.

Confessions: A confession is, in theory, a voluntary admission of having perpetrated a criminal act. However, in the days before the tape recording of witness and suspect statements, many 'confessions' were suspected of having been written by police officers, with the implication that these confessions were fabricated. However, just because police officers wrote out a confession does not mean that it was fabricated, even if it contains examples of **police register**.

Copyright infringement: See 'Plagiarism'.

Corpus (plural, *corpora*): Literally 'body', in this case a body of language assembled for research purposes.

Corpus linguistics: The study of the properties of language by the use of large banks of data of language. The Bank of English at the University of Birmingham has the world's largest language corpus. The British National Corpus at Oxford University is another very large language corpus (over 100 million words). More and more, however, linguists are seeking to develop specialized language corpora.

Cusum: See 'Qsum'.

Daubert: See 'Expert evidence tests'.

Duty to court: All witnesses have a duty of truth to the court, but expert witnesses have extra duties, such as the requirement to be impartial, to avoid advocacy, to report results which may go against their own expert view and so on. Unlike ordinary witnesses, expert witnesses may give their opinion on matters within their expertise.

Exemplar texts: An exemplar text is a sample of a candidate author's use of language.

Expert evidence tests: The test whereby a court decides whether (i) an expert is qualified to give evidence and whether that evidence should be admitted, (ii) the method/s used by the expert are suitable, effective and open to an external test such as peer review or statistical significance tests, and (iii) the tests undertaken by an expert are relevant, appropriate, and accurately carried out. In the United States of America there are two main expert evidence tests: (a) the Frye test where the test is whether the expert is appropriately qualified and the method used has been either subject to peer review or is accepted in the scientific community and (b) the Daubert test where the test is whether the method used has been subject to critical testing (such as falsification, statistical significance, etc). This is just a brief summary – there is more detail on these two expert evidence tests on the Internet.

Expert witness: A witness who, through education, training or experience, possesses a specialized knowledge beyond that of the lay person, and is therefore qualified to give an opinion to a court on a matter about which the members of the court (judge, jury, lawyers) would be unable to form an accurate opinion on their own. Every court decides for itself whether to allow an expert witness to testify. See 'Evidence tests'.

False confessions: See 'Confessions'.

Forensic text types: A forensic text is any text which is the subject of police investigation or criminal procedure. Types include ransom demands, suicide notes, hate mail, covert police recordings, threat texts and so on.

Frye: See 'Expert evidence tests'.

Function word: A word which has a grammatical function only and contains little or no content, for example, 'the', 'of', 'any' and so on. See also 'Lexical word'.

Hapax legomen: A word which occurs only once in a text, also known as a *hapax* (plural, *hapax legomena*).

Hate mail: An anonymous letter, email or mobile (cell) phone text which is designed to cause fear or distress to its recipient or to impact negatively on the reputation of a third party – see also 'Malicious communication'.

Illocution: The intended meaning of a speaker (or writer) as opposed to the surface meaning or the meaning taken by the hearer (or reader). See also 'Perlocution' and 'Locution' and 'Speech act theory'.

Impartiality: The attitude of mind of the expert witness to be fair and equitable in his/her dealings with evidence: to report evidence which may contradict their own opinion; to consider alternative hypotheses; to avoid taking sides in a case; to avoid allowing one's own view of punishment methods (such as capital punishment) to influence one's opinion; to arrive at one's opinion independently; not to bias presentation of results; to avoid rhetoric when giving evidence; to answer questions truthfully without prevarication. The expert witness should not attempt to form, and certainly should not express, an opinion on the guilt or innocence of a defendant.

Inflection: the morphological attachment of a prefix, suffix or word ending, for example, '-ed' to indicate past tense in English, or, for example, the prefix 'un', attached to a word such as 'screw'. In general, if a word cannot take an inflection it is a function word. See 'Function word'.

Inherited properties: Some human properties, such as fingerprints, are inherited, but language is not. It is socially acquired. See 'Acquired property'.

IPA: The International Phonetic Association. A group of leading phoneticians who concern themselves with the sound systems of all of the world's known languages and their transcription. The IPA Chart, which records most of the phones in the world's known languages, is an essential reference for anyone interested in or working in phonetics. The IPA Chart can be used for transcribing any language.

Lexical density: The percentage of lexical words in a text.

Lexical word: A word with content or meaning, for example, 'happy', 'coal', 'walk' and so on. Lexical words can usually be modified – for example, a noun can take a plural, an adjective can take a prefix (happy, *un*happy) and so on. Function words cannot be modified. See also 'Function word' and 'Inflection'.

Linguist: one who studies linguistics. However, in some courts a linguist is the term used to refer to an interpreter or translator.

Linguistics: the systematic, scientific study of language.

Locution: The apparent surface meaning of a word or utterance, contrasted with 'Perlocution' and 'Illocution'. See also 'Speech act theory'.

Malicious communication: A communication by any means (written, spoken, or by telephone) designed to cause fear or distress to its recipient, or to spread a false report about danger, such as a hoax threat or a fire, or to damage the reputation of another.

Mean sentence length: The average number of words per sentence in a given text, usually to one decimal place, for example, 15.9.

Mean word length: The average number of letters or characters per word in a text. Calculated by first discounting all punctuation marks. Dates (excluding the day of the week) are generally treated as one word, a sum of money such as £300.00 is also usually treated as one word, unless written as, for example 'three hundred pounds'. Mean word length is usually given to two decimal places. For example, a mean word length of 3.54 would not be considered significantly different from 3.69, but would be considered significantly different from, say, 4.52 (providing that the number of words being measured across the two texts or excerpts was sufficient for the difference to be worth considering).

Memory and language: Human memory for language is limited. We can typically remember (unless we make a conscious effort to memorize) strings of no more than six or seven words in length. This has been an issue in a number of trials involving several witnesses producing allegedly identical words of perpetrators (see Ice Cream Wars appeal on the Internet).

Morpheme: the minimum grammatical unit of a language, for example, in the word dog there are two morphemes, dog and -s. Neither of these morphemes can be reduced further. Morphology is the study of the system of morphemes in a language. It is now largely the domain of those studying syntax (see 'Syntax' below).

Perlocution: The meaning taken by a hearer or reader with regard to a word or utterance. Contrasts with 'Illocution' and 'Locution'. See also 'Illocution' and 'Locution' and 'Speech act theory'.

Phoneme: the minimum contrastive sound unit of a language, *e.g.* /b/, /k/, *etc.* English has about 44 phonemes depending on the dialect or language variety under discussion. Phoneticians (people who study phonetics and phonology) usually write a phoneme within a pair of forward slashes, *e.g.* /z/ is the phoneme representing the letter 's' in the word 'present'. Some phoneme symbols represent two letters, for example, /ʤ/ represents the 'dg' sound in the word 'edge'. Although 'dg' consists of two letters, it is one sound, that is, one phoneme – hence one phonetic symbol.

Phonetics: the study of the sounds of a language, usually written in phonetic symbols (see IPA).

Phonology: the study of the sound system of a language.

Plagiarism: the activity of using other people's written or spoken language to originate a text without proper acknowledgement to the source. There are three types of plagiarism: *literal plagiarism*, *mosaic plagiarism* and *conceptual plagiarism*. Literal plagiarism is the word for word adoption of another's text, while mosaic plagiarism is the attempt to disguise the source of the text by changing grammatical structures, word order or some of the vocabulary. Conceptual plagiarism is the theft of ideas and their mode of expression within the context of the work being plagiarised. Attempting to prove conceptual plagiarism is very difficult. Note: plagiarism is not an offence, but copyright infringement is (in the civil courts). Copyright infringement is any of the above activities in the context of a work which the plagiarist (or infringer) has published.

Plagiarist: one who plagiarizes (see plagiarism).

Police register: The style or dialect of language used by police officers in the course of writing reports or statements.

Pragmatics: the study of the application of speaker–addressee context, as well as external contextual factors, to communication, closely related to 'semantics' (see below).

Qsum: A statistical method designed to test an exemplar text for authorship. It was discredited in UK courts by several linguists and psychologists.

Questioned text (also 'suspect text'): a text whose authorship is unknown, or whose authenticity is doubted, or which is the subject of civil or criminal inquiry.

Semantics: the study of meaning, either theoretically or empirically. Semantics deals with truth conditions, sense and reference and the (broadly) metaphoric relations between words (such as metonymy, meronymy, etc).

Speaker commitment: See 'Statement analysis'.

Spectrogram: A spectrogram is a visual recording of certain parameters of sound, especially the amplitude and intensity of the voice at certain frequencies. Can be useful in voice identification. See 'Voice identification'.

Speech act theory: The branch of linguistics which deals with how speech (and writing) perform acts, for example 'I declare you man and wife', 'I bequeath my estate to . . .' and so on. Other examples include warning, promising, threatening and so on. This line of thinking in linguistics was developed by J. L. Austin and published in his book 'How to do things with words' (1962).

Statement analysis: The analysis of language to determine veracity. This is not an entirely accepted discipline within linguistics as yet. At the time of writing researchers are examining several possible models of language in an effort to gain credibility for this subject area. One possible model is the development of ways of testing for speaker commitment, that is, the degree to which a speaker/writer is seen to be committed to a text.

Style marker: A feature of a text used to measure style, for example the way a person uses punctuation, measurement of certain function words, mean word length, mean sentence length and so on. See also 'Text measures'.

Syntax: the study of the grammar of the sentence. In traditional syntax, as proposed by Noam Chomsky and his followers, the focus of the study (and much of linguistics at the time) was to understand how native speakers of a language acquired competence in the language, by which was meant the ability to generate and understand a potentially infinite number of sentences.

Text measures: attributes of a text which can be measured, for example, text length (the number of words in a text), lexical density – the number of lexical words divided by the total number of words and so on. See also 'Style markers'.

Veracity analysis: See 'Statement analysis'.

Voice identification: The process whereby a phonetician (i.e. one who studies phonetics – the sounds of a language, and phonology – the sound system of a language) examines samples of recorded spoken language to see whether the properties of a voice present in a recording match the voice properties of a suspect. See 'Phoneme', 'Phonetics' and 'Phonology'.

INDEX